1st EDITION

Perspectives on Modern World History

The Internment of Japanese Americans

1st EDITION

Perspectives on Modern World History

The Internment of Japanese Americans

Jeff Hay

Editor

GREENHAVEN PRESS
A part of Gale, Cengage Learning

GALE
CENGAGE Learning™

Detroit • New York • San Francisco • New Haven, Conn • Waterville, Maine • London

Elizabeth Des Chenes, *Managing Editor*

© 2012 Greenhaven Press, a part of Gale, Cengage Learning.

Gale and Greenhaven Press are registered trademarks used herein under license.

For more information, contact:
Greenhaven Press
27500 Drake Rd.
Farmington Hills, MI 48331-3535
Or you can visit our Internet site at gale.cengage.com.

For product information and technology assistance, contact us at
Gale Customer Support, 1-800-877-4253.

For permission to use material from this text or product, submit all requests online at
www.cengage.com/permissions.

Further permissions questions can be e-mailed to permissionrequest@cengage.com.

Articles in Greenhaven Press anthologies are often edited for length to meet page requirements. In addition, original titles of these works are changed to clearly present the main thesis and to explicitly indicate the author's opinion. Every effort is made to ensure that Greenhaven Press accurately reflects the original intent of the authors. Every effort has been made to trace the owners of copyrighted material.

Cover image © Corbis.

LIBRARY OF CONGRESS CATALOGING-IN-PUBLICATION DATA
The internment of Japanese Americans / Jeff Hay, book editor.
   p. cm. -- (Perspectives on modern world history)
   Includes bibliographical references and index.
   ISBN 978-0-7377-5792-7 (hardcover)
1. Japanese Americans--Evacuation and relocation, 1942–1945. 2. World War, 1939–1945--Japanese Americans. 3. Japanese--United States--History. I. Hay, Jeff.
   D769.8.A6I57 2011
   940.53'1773--dc23   2011018848

Printed in the United States of America
2 3 4 5 6 7 15 14 13 12

CONTENTS

In February 1942, US president Franklin D. Roosevelt gave military commanders the ability to designate districts from which people might be excluded or find their rights limited in order to reduce the threats of sabotage and spying. His order made it possible for West Coast commanders to begin to remove Japanese Americans.

CHAPTER 2

Controversies Over Japanese American Internment

In 1983, the Supreme Court's ruling in *Hirabayashi v. United States* was overturned.

Ronald Takaki

By the end of 1942, the US government made it possible for Japanese Americans who were citizens to serve in the armed forces during World War II. More than thirty thousand did so, some claiming it was the best way for them to show their devotion to their country.

W. Dale Nelson

Internees who refused to be drafted into the armed services recall their experiences. Even though some faced terms in military prisons, they continued to hold that their constitutional rights as citizens were being violated by relocation and internment.

CHAPTER 3   Personal Narratives

Yoshiko Uchida

An author describes how, in the aftermath of Japan's attack on the US naval base at Pearl Harbor, Hawaii, on December 7, 1941, her family faced an increasingly shaky future. Her father was quickly detained as a potential enemy sympathizer.

FOREWORD

"History cannot give us a program for the future, but it can give us a fuller understanding of ourselves, and of our common humanity, so that we can better face the future."

—Robert Penn Warren,
American poet and novelist

The history of each nation is punctuated by momentous events that represent turning points for that nation, with an impact felt far beyond its borders. These events—displaying the full range of human capabilities, from violence, greed, and ignorance to heroism, courage, and strength—are nearly always complicated and multifaceted. Any student of history faces the challenge of grasping the many strands that constitute such world-changing events as wars, social movements, and environmental disasters. But understanding these significant historic events can be enhanced by exposure to a variety of perspectives, whether of people involved intimately or of ones observing from a distance of miles or years. Understanding can also be increased by learning about the controversies surrounding such events and exploring hot-button issues from multiple angles. Finally, true understanding of important historic events involves knowledge of the events' human impact—of the ways such events affected people in their everyday lives—all over the world.

Perspectives on Modern World History examines global historic events from the twentieth-century onward by presenting analysis and observation from numerous vantage points. Each volume offers high school, early college level, and general interest readers a thematically arranged anthology of previously published materials that address a major historical event, with an emphasis on international coverage. Each volume opens with background information on the event, then presents the controversies surrounding that event, and concludes with first-person narratives from people who lived through the event or were affected by it. By providing primary sources from the time of the event, as well as relevant commentary surrounding the event, this series can be used to inform debate, help develop critical thinking skills, increase global awareness, and enhance an understanding of international perspectives on history.

Material in each volume is selected from a diverse range of sources, including journals, magazines, newspapers, nonfiction books, personal narratives, speeches, congressional testimony, government documents, pamphlets, organization newsletters, and position papers. Articles taken from these sources are carefully edited and introduced to provide context and background. Each volume of Perspectives on Modern World History includes an array of views on events of global significance. Much of the material comes from international sources and from US sources that provide extensive international coverage.

Each volume in the Perspectives on Modern World History series also includes:

- A full-color **world map**, offering context and geographic perspective.
- An annotated **table of contents** that provides a brief summary of each essay in the volume.
- An **introduction** specific to the volume topic.
- For each viewpoint, a brief **introduction** that has notes about the author and source of the viewpoint, and that provides a summary of its main points.
- Full-color **charts**, **graphs**, **maps**, and other visual representations.

- Informational **sidebars** that explore the lives of key individuals, give background on historical events, or explain scientific or technical concepts.
- A **glossary** that defines key terms, as needed.
- A **chronology** of important dates preceding, during, and immediately following the event.
- A **bibliography** of additional books, periodicals, and websites for further research.
- A comprehensive **subject index** that offers access to people, places, and events cited in the text.

Perspectives on Modern World History is designed for a broad spectrum of readers who want to learn more about not only history but also current events, political science, government, international relations, and sociology—students doing research for class assignments or debates, teachers and faculty seeking to supplement course materials, and others wanting to improve their understanding of history. Each volume of Perspectives on Modern World History is designed to illuminate a complicated event, to spark debate, and to show the human perspective behind the world's most significant happenings of recent decades.

INTRODUCTION

On April 23, 1942, a strange headline appeared in the *San Diego Union*, a major newspaper in that Southern California city. It read, "Evacuation 'Glorious Holiday' to Many Jap[anese]." The story that followed reported on a visit made by a US government official to a local chapter of the League of Women Voters, where questions were raised as to what was happening to the Japanese families who lived in the area. The meeting's attendees learned that Japanese residents had been sent away to relocation centers in inland areas, away from the Pacific Coast. But rather than consider this an attack on their freedoms, the official argued, some of the evacuees thought this a "glorious holiday." Two days later, seeming to follow up on the official's claim, a second headline read "Japanese Enjoying 'Vacation.'"

Few in the years since would agree with the anonymous official from 1942. What the *San Diego Union* reported as a "holiday" or "vacation" has instead become commonly considered one of the disgraceful episodes of twentieth-century US history, a period in which the constitutional rights of its citizens were plainly violated.

In 1942, more than a hundred thousand residents of Japanese descent were sent away from their homes, farms, and businesses on the West Coast to inland internment camps. The majority of the evacuees were US citizens, and none were ever formally accused of a crime. They were asked, on very short notice, to sell or lease land or buildings, to sell or give away their property, and to pack only a few belongings. For many, their first stop was a temporary facility such as a horse racetrack or the livestock areas of a county fairground. While the evacuees adjusted to their new reality, a government organization known as the

War Relocation Authority was busy establishing permanent internment camps, often in isolated, desolate areas. The process moved quickly; most received their original evacuation orders in March and April 1942 and were in internment camps by the fall of that year.

The US government's decision to relocate Japanese residents living on the West Coast came from events following a surprise attack on the US naval base at Pearl Harbor, Hawaii, on December 7, 1941. The attack resulted in the deaths of more than twenty-three hundred servicemen and in the United States' entry into World War II. It was carried out by forces of Imperial Japan seeking to end American influence in the Pacific Ocean and Asia. By all accounts, the attack was a major military success, and many Americans feared that an attack on California, Oregon, or Washington would quickly follow.

The majority of US residents of Japanese descent lived in those three West Coast states, or in the Hawaiian Islands. Fears arose that members of these communities might be engaged in spying for Imperial Japan, or planning for sabotage as part of a larger Japanese attack. These fears were unfounded, as no plans for spying or sabotage were ever uncovered, but they were felt deeply at the time. To guard against any such activity, and for the sake of larger military security, President Franklin D. Roosevelt issued Executive Order 9066 on February 19, 1942. The order allowed military officials to designate "military areas" along the West Coast from which certain people could be excluded out of military necessity. Lieutenant General John L. Dewitt, head of the military's Western Command, selected several such military zones and singled out Japanese residents for exclusion. Most people on the West Coast agreed with DeWitt's plans. In addition to general war fears, some observers and officials simply questioned the loyalty of Japanese residents while, more insidiously, a few hoped to gain economic advantage by ending competition from Japanese farmers or businessmen. Still others feared race riots, and thought that the Japanese should be sent away for their own safety, regardless of whether they were US citizens.

Most of the relocated were US citizens, second-generation Japanese Americans born on US soil. The Japanese population in the United States at that time could be divided into two generations, as the Japanese themselves did: the Issei and Nisei. The Issei were first-generation Japanese immigrants, generally having arrived in the United States in the late 1800s and early 1900s. Laws in place in this era made it impossible for the Issei to achieve full US citizenship, although they could live, work, and own property legally. Since they were not citizens, the Issei could be designated as "enemy aliens" during World War II, as were many German or Italian residents who were not US citizens.

The flow of new Japanese immigrants mostly stopped following a so-called "Gentlemen's Agreement" between the United States and Japan in 1907 and 1908. The major exceptions were the "picture brides." Few of the earlier immigrants, mostly men, had married, and since the Gentlemen's Agreement allowed for the immigration of immediate family members, thousands of Issei entered into arranged marriages with women in Japan whom they only knew from photographs. The women then travelled to the United States to meet their husbands. The children of this generation were the Nisei, or second-generation Japanese Americans.

Since they were born on US soil, the Nisei had a constitutional guarantee of American citizenship, and they could not be designated as enemy aliens. The majority, furthermore, were English-speaking and culturally "Americanized," holding no loyalty to or much interest in Japan. General DeWitt's relocation orders, however, did not differentiate between citizens or noncitizens; they did not even, for the most part, accuse any enemy aliens of actual anti-American activity. Whether Issei or Nisei,

Japanese Americans were simply forced to leave their homes for resettlement in what many of them referred to as concentration camps. Legal challenges to the relocation orders and interment camps were upheld by the US Supreme Court, which determined that, in wartime, military necessity took precedence over the citizenship rights of Japanese Americans.

The War Relocation Authority established ten relocation centers: Manzanar and Tule Lake in California; Poston and Gila River in Arizona; Granada in Colorado; Heart Mountain in Wyoming; Minidoka in Idaho; Topaz in Idaho; and Rohwer and Jerome in Arkansas. These locations were often isolated and suffered from harsh climates. Facilities in the camps were hastily built and fairly primitive. Families lived in blocks of barracks, sharing bathrooms, kitchens, and cafeterias. The camps were surrounded by barbed wire and maintained armed guards, making it impossible to leave without permission. As the weeks and months passed, the evacuees made the best of their situation by improving their barracks, establishing gardens, and staging sporting events, dances, and other activities. The War Relocation Authority also, eventually, opened schools in the camps and gave some evacuees a role in running them. Still, unless they had special permission, internees were not permitted to leave the camps.

One way in which to gain special permission was to move eastward, away from the military exclusion zones. Many Nisei chose to do so, and church organizations as well as other benevolent groups helped them find jobs and housing, mostly in Midwestern states. However, to do so often meant leaving family members in the camps. The elder Issei were not given this option, so many people not only had to leave their brothers and sisters but also their parents behind.

A second way to gain release from the camps was to join the US armed services, another option open only to Nisei. Some Hawaiian Nisei had, in fact, served in the military from the beginning of World War II. (Japanese Americans in Hawaii were never subjected to relocation on any large scale.) Mainland Nisei were at first forbidden from joining, but intensive lobbying, often by Japanese American interest groups or even inmates of the camps themselves, brought about a change in policy. In early 1943, the US Army formed a new unit, eventually known as the 442nd Regimental Combat Team, which was to be made up of mostly Nisei soldiers and to take part in the war in Europe against Germany and Italy. In addition to volunteering, young Nisei men could be drafted into the military. Here again, however, they were subject to requirements other Americans did not have to meet, such as filling out a loyalty questionnaire asked of all adult evacuees in February 1943. Satisfactory answers meant that a young Nisei man could either volunteer or be drafted into the armed services. The 442nd went on to become the most highly decorated army unit of its size in World War II, as Nisei soldiers took very seriously the idea of proving their loyalty.

The end of the war did not mean an easy return to normalcy for evacuees. The internment camps were closed in 1945, the year the United States defeated Imperial Japan and its allies in World War II, or in early 1946. The people freed from the camps now found their lives uncertain; families were separated, with younger people often scattered around the country or even still overseas with the armed forces. Many of those who returned to their West Coast homes found their farms or businesses no longer viable and neighbors hostile. In most cases it took years before Japanese American families were able to reestablish themselves, with very little help from the government. One major change, however, came in 1952, when Issei, along with other Asian immigrants, finally gained the ability to become US citizens.

Led by activist Nisei as well as the younger Sansei, or third generation, Japanese American leaders actively began to seek justice for World War II-era wrongs in the 1970s. Their efforts have been successful in a wide range of areas. In the 1980s, the Supreme Court's decisions upholding exclusion and relocation on the grounds of wartime necessity were overturned. Some of the camps, notably Manzanar in California, have been recognized as important historical sites. Meanwhile, a varied group of Japanese American organizations and individuals, including some veterans of the 442nd Regimental Combat Team who had been elected to the US Congress, achieved a major victory in 1988. That year, a civil liberties act was enacted in which the government offered a full apology to survivors of the camps as well as a sum of $20,000 each in compensation. The measure offered at least a little recognition that what Japanese Americans had experienced in World War II was hardly a "vacation" or "holiday," as the *San Diego Union* carelessly reported back in April 1942. It was instead a period of upheaval, privation, injustice, and great uncertainty.

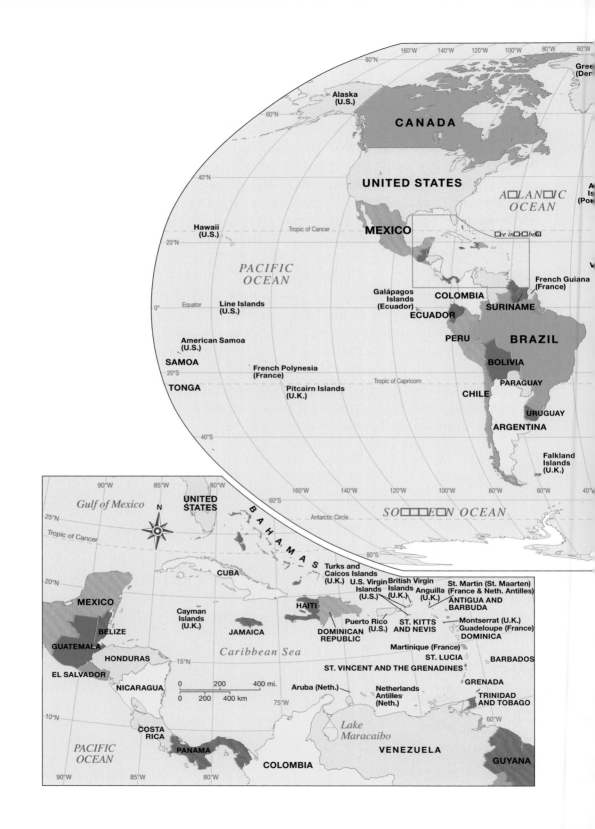

160°W 140°W 120°W 100°W 80°W 60°W

80°N

Gree
(Der

60°N

Alaska
(U.S.)

CANADA

40°N

UNITED STATES

A☐LAN☐IC
OCEAN

A
Is
(Po

Hawaii
(U.S.)

Tropic of Cancer

MEXICO

☐ee in☐☐be☐☐

20°N

PACIFIC
OCEAN

French Guiana
(France)

Galápagos
Islands
(Ecuador)

COLOMBIA

SURINAME

0° Equator Line Islands
(U.S.)

ECUADOR

American Samoa
(U.S.)

PERU

BRAZIL

SAMOA

BOLIVIA

20°S

French Polynesia
(France)

Tropic of Capricorn

PARAGUAY

TONGA

Pitcairn Islands
(U.K.)

CHILE

URUGUAY

ARGENTINA

40°S

Falkland
Islands
(U.K.)

160°W 140°W 120°W 100°W 80°W 60°W 40°

60°S

Antarctic Circle

SO☐☐☐E☐N OCEAN

80°S

90°W 85°W 80°W

Gulf of Mexico N UNITED
STATES

B
A
H
A
M
A
S

25°N

Tropic of Cancer

CUBA

Turks and
Caicos Islands
(U.K.)

British Virgin
U.S. Virgin Islands
Islands (U.K.)
(U.S.)

Anguilla
(U.K.)

St. Martin (St. Maarten)
(France & Neth. Antilles)

ANTIGUA AND
BARBUDA

20°N

MEXICO

Cayman
Islands
(U.K.)

HAITI

JAMAICA

Puerto Rico
(U.S.)

DOMINICAN
REPUBLIC

ST. KITTS
AND NEVIS

Montserrat (U.K.)
Guadeloupe (France)

DOMINICA

BELIZE

GUATEMALA

HONDURAS

Caribbean Sea

Martinique (France)

ST. LUCIA

BARBADOS

15°N

EL SALVADOR

ST. VINCENT AND THE GRENADINES

NICARAGUA

0 200 400 mi.

0 200 400 km

75°W

Aruba (Neth.)

Netherlands
Antilles
(Neth.)

GRENADA

TRINIDAD
AND TOBAGO

10°N

COSTA
RICA

PACIFIC
OCEAN

PANAMA

Lake
Maracaibo

VENEZUELA

GUYANA

COLOMBIA

90°W 85°W 80°W 60°W

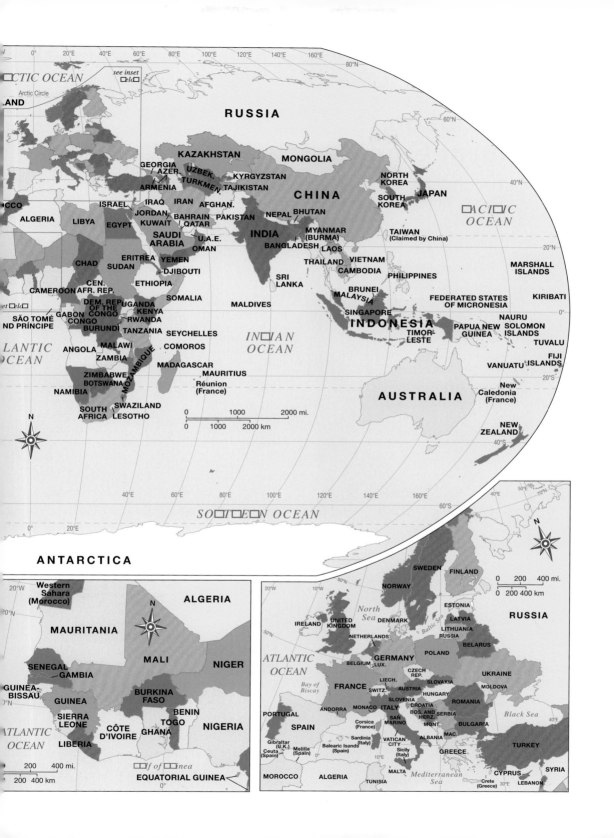

CHAPTER 1

Background on the Japanese American Internment Camps

Japanese American Internment in World War II: An Overview

Midori Takagi

In the following selection, a scholar provides an overview of the Japanese American internment camps during World War II. Beginning in 1942, Japanese Americans living on the West Coast of the United States were forced to relocate to the camps. Takagi's summary ranges from an examination of the internment order itself to a description of life in the camps to the measures taken to redress the wrongs of the camps beginning in the 1970s, some thirty years after the camps were opened. Midori Takagi is a professor of Interdisciplinary Studies at Western Washington University.

Photo on previous page: US Army medical corps personnel help an elderly Japanese woman after she collapsed during the evacuation of Bainbridge Island in Puget Sound, Washington. Three hundred persons of Japanese descent were evacuated from the island on April 1, 1942. (**Associated Press.**)

SOURCE. Midori Takagi, "Japanese American Internment Camps," *St. James Encyclopedia of Popular Culture*, 1E, Sara Pendergast and Tom Pendergast, eds. www.cengage.com. © 2000 Gale, a part of Cengage Learning, Inc. Reproduced by permission.

Between February and November 1942, nearly 120,000 West Coast residents of Japanese descent were evacuated from their homes and sent to government War Relocation Authority camps in remote areas of the West, South, and Southwest. Many of these Japanese and Japanese Americans would spend the remainder of World War II in the camps, which were located in Gila River, Arizona; Granada, Colorado; Heart Mountain, Wyoming; Jerome, Arkansas; Manzanar, California; Minidoka, Idaho; Poston, Arizona; Rohwer, Arkansas; Topaz, Utah; and Tule Lake, California. The largest camp, Tule Lake, housed nearly 19,000 internees, while Granada held about 7,000. The camps' residents lived in crudely built barracks, and ate, bathed, and washed clothes in communal facilities. Each camp was surrounded by barbed wire and guarded by armed soldiers. The first camp, Poston, opened in May, 1942. Nearly two years later the government began closing the camps starting with Jerome, in June, 1944, and ending with Tule Lake, in March, 1946.

> Each camp was surrounded by barbed wire and guarded by armed soldiers.

The Internment Order

The internment of the Issei (first generation) and the Nisei (second generation, American-born) was authorized by President Franklin D. Roosevelt through Executive Order 9066 (February 19, 1942), which sanctioned the evacuation of any and all persons from "military zones" established along the coastline. Although the federal government also viewed persons of German and Italian descent with suspicion, only residents of Japanese ancestry were forced to leave their homes.

Executive Order 9066 was a response to Japan's attack on Pearl Harbor [Hawaii] on December 7, 1941. Following the attack, government officials including U.S.

attorney general Francis Biddle, Los Angeles congress-man Leland Ford, and California attorney general Earl Warren called for securing the Issei and Nisei popula-tion. They believed that West Coast Japanese helped plan the attack on Pearl Harbor and hoped the internment would prevent further acts of disloyalty. Studies indicate, however, that anti-Japanese sentiment, which had been building on the West Coast since the late nineteenth cen-tury, played a role in the forced evacuation. These stud-ies point to the fact that only West Coast Issei and Nisei were removed—not those living in Hawaii or on the East

Hundreds of Japanese Americans salute the flag at an intern-ment camp in Heart Mountain, Wyoming. **(Time & Life Pictures/Getty Images.)**

Japanese Immigrants to the United States

People from Japan started coming to the United States in the second half of the nineteenth century. The first Japanese immigrants arrived in California in 1869, seeking to escape political turmoil in Japan. They were followed by others who went both to California and the other West Coast states of Oregon and Washington. Most newcomers started small farms, although a few settled in towns and cities.

A larger community of Japanese newcomers arose in Hawaii, which, until the 1890s, was an independent kingdom. As American businessmen tried to turn the Hawaiian Islands into a major agricultural center in the 1800s, they imported workers for the sugarcane and pineapple fields. The first of these, Chinese workers, moved out of agricultural labor as quickly as possible. To replace them, the planters looked to Japan for workers, and large numbers of Japanese immigrated to Hawaii in the last decades of the 1800s. The Hawaiian monarchy was overthrown in the 1890s and the islands became a US territory.

Japanese immigrants endured considerable prejudice, notably in California. There, an anti-Japanese movement staged vocal demonstrations in the first decade of the twentieth century and sought to deny newcomers the ability to attend public schools. To reduce tensions, US president Theodore Roosevelt and the Japanese government entered into a so-called "Gentlemen's Agreement" on the issue of further immigration. In the deal, reached in 1907, Japan agreed to stop giving passports

Coast—and that the residents calling for their removal were California nativists, laborers, and farmers, who had long viewed Japanese immigrants as social and economic threats. The 1982 report issued by the Commission on Wartime Relocation and Internment of Civilians concluded that the removal of the Issei and Nisei was not a military necessity, but occurred because of racism, wartime hysteria, and poor political leadership.

Under the direction of Lieutenant General John L. DeWitt, the Issei and Nisei were first evacuated to assembly centers at county fairgrounds and racetracks, and they were later moved to the permanent relocation camps. In to those Japanese people who wanted to go to the United States as laborers. The United States, meanwhile, agreed to only admit new Japanese immigrants if they were the immediate family members of those already in the country. One creative response among Japanese Americans was to arrange marriages. Through their families back home, many men entered into such unions and then brought their wives over. The women were known as picture brides, since photographs of their future spouses were all their hopeful grooms ever saw of them before they arrived.

These immigrants, the so-called Issei, or first-generation, could not become naturalized US citizens because of a 1790 Naturalization Act that limited the privilege to "free white persons."

Their children, however, the Nisei, were automatically US citizens thanks to the constitutional guarantee of birthright citizenship. Further Japanese immigration to the United States ended in 1924 with the passage of a broad immigration act. The measure remained in effect until 1952, effectively dividing the Japanese American community into Issei, who had no pathway to US citizenship, and Nisei, who were citizens by birth. Generational differences were also reflected in behavior; many of the Issei clung to Japanese traditions and even the language of their homeland, while the Nisei generally considered themselves quite Americanized.

some locations, such as Terminal Island in San Pedro, California, residents of Japanese descent were given as few as two days to dispose of, or store, their belongings before departing. In other areas, the evacuees had several weeks to prepare. Though the Federal Reserve Bank and the Farm Security Administration helped handle the property and belongings of the Issei and Nisei, they lost hundreds of thousands of dollars through quick sales of their homes and land at below-market prices. While in camp the evacuees suffered additional losses through vandalism, arson, and neglect of the belongings that had been stored.

LOCATION OF JAPANESE AMERICAN INTERNMENT CAMPS AND RELATED SITES

This map shows sites in the western United States associated with the relocation of Japanese Americans during World War II.

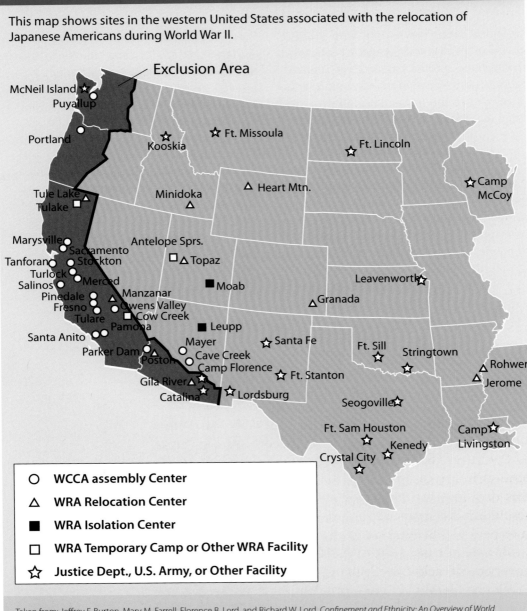

Taken from: Jeffrey F. Burton, Mary M. Farrell, Florence B. Lord, and Richard W. Lord, *Confinement and Ethnicity: An Overview of World War II Japanese American Relocation Sites*. National Park Service, 1999.

Relocation and Loss

Life in the camps proved difficult. Internees had lost their jobs, social networks, and educational opportunities and were removed from "mainstream" life. Angered by the loss of their rights and freedom, and bitter towards the U.S. government, internees sometimes directed their hostility toward one another. In some camps riots broke out during clashes between pro-Japanese and pro-American factions. A loyalty test administered by the War Relocation Administration also helped to factionalize the evacuees. As a result of the turbulence, hundreds of young Nisei left the camps when the opportunity appeared. Colleges such as Oberlin in Ohio sponsored Nisei students, allowing them to relocate and resume their education. Christian churches arranged for Nisei to work in homes and offices located in the South and Midwest. In addition, more than 1,000 men joined the U.S. military forces and served in the all-Nisei 442nd Regimental Combat Team.

> It was not until the 1970s that branches of the U.S. government acknowledged any wrongdoing.

Although many evacuees protested the removal, four individuals, Fred T. Korematsu, Mitsuye Endo, Minoru Yasui, and Gordon K. Hirabayashi, challenged the constitutionality of the relocation order through the courts. Initially all four petitions were denied. But in December of 1944 the U.S. Supreme Court decided that Endo's detention in the camps violated her civil rights. Following this decision, in January of 1945, the War Department rescinded the evacuation orders and arranged for the internees to leave the camps.

It was not until the 1970s that branches of the U.S. government acknowledged any wrongdoing. In 1976, President Gerald R. Ford proclaimed that the evacuation was wrong. The 1982 commission report and its condemnation of the relocation sent an even stronger message. In 1983, Fred Korematsu, Gordon Hirabayashi, and Minoru Yasui refiled their petitions, which the court granted. The change in political tenor encouraged the Nisei and Sansei (third generation) to seek redress and reparations for the forced relocation. Their organizing efforts culminated in September of 1987, when the U.S. House of Representatives formally apologized to the former evacuees and provided $12 billion as compensation.

Many Factors Influenced the Government's Decision to Open Internment Camps

David M. Kennedy

In the following selection, a historian describes the context in which US officials made the decision to intern Japanese Americans living on the West Coast. His emphasis is on the emergence of "war-fueled hysteria" in the weeks following the attack on the US naval base at Pearl Harbor, Hawaii, by Japan's navy on December 7, 1941. Such feelings developed even though officials such as General John L. DeWitt, who was in charge of defenses along the West Coast, and Attorney General Francis Biddle initially rejected any idea of evacuating Japanese Americans. This hysteria was fed by fears inspired by Japan's rapid military advances in Asia and

SOURCE. David M. Kennedy, "The Cauldron on the Home Front," *The American People in World War II: Freedom from Fear: Part II*, Oxford University Press, 1999, pp. 323–327. © 1999 by David M. Kennedy. Reproduced by permission of Oxford University Press, Inc.

the Pacific over that winter, and by a rising suspicion that some Japanese Americans were engaged in spying—suspicions which, the author notes, had little basis in fact. Newspaper and radio columnists added to the rising hysteria, as did West Coast farmers' groups who wanted to remove Japanese American competition. The recipient of a Pulitzer Prize and the author of many books on US history, David M. Kennedy is the Donald J. MacLachlan Professor of History at Stanford University.

Following the attack on Pearl Harbor, Hawaii passed under martial law, the writ of habeas corpus [which prevents unlawful imprisonment] was suspended, and the military police took several hundred suspected spies and saboteurs of Japanese extraction into custody. But the very size of the Japanese community in Hawaii (nearly half the territory's population, and its vital importance to the islands' economy, foreclosed any thought of wholesale evacuation. The mainland community, however, was proportionately much smaller (in California, barely 1 percent of the population), more economically marginal and socially isolated, and long buffeted by racist pressures. The mainland Japanese for the most part kept warily to themselves, many of them toiling with exemplary efficiency on their family fruit and vegetable farms. Insular and quiescent, they were also internally riven by age and legal status. Their elders, the forty thousand first-generation immigrant Japanese, or Issei, were generally over the age of fifty and debarred from citizenship by the Immigration Restriction Act of 1924, a statutory impediment that perversely exposed them to the accusation that as non-citizens they were poorly assimilated into American society. A majority of their children, the eighty thousand second-generation Nisei, were under the age of eighteen. Born in the United States, they were also citizens. Alien and citizen alike, the peculiarly vulnerable Pacific Coast Japanese community was about to feel the full wrath of war-fueled hysteria.

At First, Calm

Curiously, no clamor for wholesale reprisals against the mainland Japanese arose in the immediate aftermath of the Pearl Harbor attack. The *Los Angeles Times* soberly editorialized on December 8 that most of the Japanese on the Coast were "good Americans, born and educated as such," and serenely foresaw that there would be "no riots, no mob law." General John L. DeWitt, chief of the army's Western Defense Command, at first dismissed loose talk of mass evacuations as "damned nonsense."

> Government surveillance, ongoing since 1935, had identified some two thousand potentially subversive persons in the Japanese community.

He condemned any broadside assaults on the rights of the American-born Nisei. "An American citizen, after all, is an American citizen," he declared. Individual arrests were another matter. Government surveillance, ongoing since 1935, had identified some two thousand potentially subversive persons in the Japanese community. Along with fourteen thousand German and Italian security risks nationwide, they were quietly rounded up in the last days of 1941. But those individual detentions stopped well short of wholesale incarcerations. "I was determined," Attorney General Francis Biddle wrote, "to avoid mass internment, and the persecution of aliens that had characterized the First World War."

In fact, the immigrants whose loyalty had been questioned during World War I had then been freshly arrived and seemed to many observers unarguably alien. But by 1941 those older European groups were settled communities, well assimilated, their patriotism as well as their political loyalty actively cultivated by [US president Franklin D.] Roosevelt's New Deal. Though a surprising six hundred thousand Italians—more than 10 percent of the entire Italian-American community— remained Italian citizens and were automatically labeled

UNITED STATES WAR RELOCATION AUTHORITY
CITIZEN'S INDEFINITE LEAVE

This is to certify that

Furuya, Kameyo

a United States citizen residing

within Colo. River Relocation

Area is allowed to leave such area on 6/14

19 44 and, subject to the terms of the regulations of the War Relocation Authority relating to the issuance of leave for departure from a relocation area and subject to any special conditions or restrictions set forth on the reverse side hereof, to enjoy leave of indefinite duration. The holder's first destination is South Haven, Mich.

19567 Acting (Project Director)

Japanese American internees could often leave their camps, provided they had official permission, traveled only to areas outside restricted military zones, and carried special documents. (Amber Tiffany/Furuya family, San Diego, CA.)

"enemy aliens" after [Italian dictator Benito] Mussolini's declaration of war [on December 11, 1941], Roosevelt instructed Biddle to cancel that designation in a joyfully received announcement at Carnegie Hall, shrewdly delivered on Columbus Day 1942, just weeks before the congressional elections.

War Fears on the West Coast

The Japanese were not so fortunate. As war rumors took wing in the weeks following Pearl Harbor, sobriety gave way to anxiety, then to a rising cry for draconian action against the Japanese on the West Coast. Inflammatory and invariably false reports of Japanese attacks on the American mainland flashed through coastal communities. Eleanor Roosevelt's airplane, en route to Los Angeles on the evening of the Pearl Harbor attack, was grounded in the Midwest while the first lady telephoned Washington to check a radio message that San Francisco was under bombardment. Painters at Stanford University blacked out the skylight of the library's main reading room so that it could not serve as a beacon to enemy pilots. Carpenters hammered up dummy aircraft plants in Los Angeles to decoy Japanese bombers away from the real factories. Athletic officials moved the tradi- tional New Year's Day football classic from the Rose Bowl in Pasadena, California; the game was played in- stead in North Carolina, presumably

> Japan's astonishing string of victories in the Pacific further unsettled American public opinion.

safe from Japanese attack. Japan's astonishing string of victories in the Pacific further unsettled American pub- lic opinion. Hong Kong fell on December 2, Manila on January 2, Singapore on January 25.

The release at the end of January of a government investigation of the Pearl Harbor attack proved the de- cisive blow. The report, prepared by Supreme Court Justice Owen J. Roberts, alleged without documentation that Hawaii-based espionage agents, including Japanese- American citizens, had abetted [Japanese admiral Chu- ichi] Nagumo's strike force. Two days later, DeWitt reported "a tremendous volume of public opinion now developing against the Japanese of all classes, that is aliens and non-aliens." DeWitt himself, described by Biddle as having a "tendency to reflect the views of the last man to whom he talked," soon succumbed to Rumor's siren. He wildly declared to an incredulous Justice Department of- ficial that every ship sailing out of the Columbia [River, separating Oregon and Washington] had been attacked by submarines guided by clandestine radio operators near the river's mouth. When evidence of actual attacks failed to materialize, DeWitt invoked the tortured logic that the very absence of any sabotage activity on the West Coast proved the existence of an organized, disci- plined conspiracy in the Japanese community, cunningly withholding its blow until it could be struck with lethal effect. In February the respected columnist Walter Lippmann alleged that military authorities had evidence of radio communications between "the enemy at sea and enemy agents on land"—a charge that FBI director J. Edgar Hoover had already advised Biddle was utterly without foundation. A radio technician from the Federal Communications Commission reviewed DeWitt's "evidence" of electronic signals and declared it hogwash. All 760 of DeWitt's suspicious radio transmissions could be accounted for, and not one involved espionage. "Frankly," the technician concluded, "I have never seen an organization [the US Army's Western Defense Command] that was so hopeless to cope with radio intelligence requirements. The personnel is unskilled and untrained. Most are privates who can read only ten words a minute. . . . It's pathetic to say the least."

Rising Fears

But by this time facts were no protection against the building gale of fear and prejudice. "Nobody's constitutional rights," Lippmann magisterially intoned, "include the right to reside and do business on a battlefield." Lippmann's colleague Westbrook Pegler echoed him less elegantly a few days later: "The Japanese in California should be under armed guard to the last man and woman right now," Pegler wrote in his widely read column, "and to hell with habeas corpus until the danger is over." Unapologetically racist voices also joined the chorus. "We're charged with wanting to get rid of the Japs for selfish reasons," a leader of California's Grower-Shipper Vegetable Association declared. "We might as well be honest. We do. It's a question of whether the white man

> It was impossible, [General DeWitt] claimed, to distinguish the loyal from the disloyal in the peculiarly alien and inscrutable Japanese community.

Imperial Japan and World War II in the Pacific and Asia

On December 7, 1941, ships and aircraft of the Imperial Japanese Navy launched a surprise attack on the US naval base at Pearl Harbor in Hawaii. The attack resulted in the deaths of twenty-four hundred people and the sinking or damaging of many US warships. American leaders responded with a quick declaration of war against Japan (Japan's allies, Germany and Italy, declared war on the United States shortly after) and, eventually, the relocation of Japanese Americans living on the West Coast of the United States to internment camps.

Japan's Pearl Harbor attack was part of a larger plan that the nation's leaders had begun devising in the 1930s. They hoped to create a "Greater East Asia Co-prosperity Sphere" under Japanese domination. In this, Japan would either subdue or force the cooperation of other Asian peoples. Their territories could then supply raw materials to feed Japan's industries and cheap labor to produce food and other goods. The process began in 1931, when Japan occupied the region of Manchuria, north of China. It continued with an invasion of China proper in 1937.

But for Japan's vision to be fully achieved, its armed forces had to deal with the Western colonial powers that controlled Southeast Asia. Great Britain had colonized Malaysia and Singapore, France maintained a territory known as Indochina (the modern nations of Vietnam, Laos, and Cambodia), and the Netherlands controlled what is today Indonesia. Even the United States maintained a major possession in the Philippines, where there were a number of US military installations.

Japan's plans received a boost in 1940, when its ally Nazi Germany conquered France and the Netherlands and threatened the survival of Britain. Japan's leaders understood that with such threats at home, the European powers could do little to protect their Asian colonies. The major remaining obstacle was the United States, most notably the US Pacific fleet. If Japan could destroy or marginalize the US Navy in the Pacific, very little stood in the way of it pursuing its imperial goals. The Pearl Harbor attack was intended to accomplish this.

Although surprise attacks were common in Japanese military history, the move against Pearl Harbor was a complete shock to Americans, who had believed that an attack, if it came, would likely target the Philippines. The shock was reinforced by rapid Japanese advances in Southeast Asia over the winter of 1941–42. In this environment, many Americans feared a Japanese attack on the West Coast of the United States was imminent and that Japan was unstoppable.

lives on the Pacific Coast or the brown man." Prodded by such sentiments, in early February 1942 DeWitt officially requested authority to remove all Japanese from the West Coast. It was impossible, he claimed, to distinguish the loyal from the disloyal in the peculiarly alien and inscrutable Japanese community. The only remedy was wholesale evacuation. The same man who had said a month earlier, "An American citizen, after all, is an American citizen," now announced, "A Jap's a Jap. . . . It makes no difference whether he is an American citizen or not. . . . I don't want any of them."

Executive Order 9066 Clears the Path for Japanese American Internment

Franklin D. Roosevelt

The internment of Japanese Americans was made possible by the following Executive Order, issued by US president Franklin D. Roosevelt on February 19, 1942. Thinking that there was a risk of sabotage or spying activity on the West Coast, Roosevelt gave military commanders the ability to designate "military areas" from which certain people could be excluded. The order did not mention Japanese Americans specifically. Any population that was "excluded," meanwhile, was to be housed and cared for under the responsibility of the Secretary of War (now Secretary of Defense). In the months that followed, General John L. DeWitt, head of the Western Defense Command, designated the Pacific Coast of the United States as a military area from which Japanese Americans needed to be removed.

SOURCE. Franklin D. Roosevelt, "Transcript of Executive Order 9066: Resulting in the Relocation of Japanese (1942)," Ourdocuments .gov, February 19, 1942.

Whereas the successful prosecution of the war requires very possible protection against espionage and against sabotage to national-defense material, national-defense premises, and national-defense utilities . . .

Now, therefore, by virtue of the authority vested in me as President of the United States, and Commander in Chief of the Army and Navy, I hereby authorize and direct the Secretary of War [now Secretary of Defense] and the Military Commanders whom he may from time to time designate, whenever he or any designated Commander deems such action necessary or desirable, to prescribe military areas in such places and of such extent as he or the appropriate Military Commander may determine, from which any or all persons may be excluded, and with respect to which, the right of any person to enter, remain in, or leave shall be subject to whatever restrictions the Secretary of War or the appropriate Military Commander may impose in his discretion. The Secretary of War is hereby authorized to provide for residents of any such area who are excluded therefrom, such transportation, food, shelter, and other accommodations as may be necessary, in the judgment of the Secretary of War or the said Military Commander, and until other arrangements are made, to accomplish the purpose of this order. The designation of military areas in any region or locality shall supersede designations of prohibited and restricted areas by the Attorney General under the Proclamations of December 7 and 8, 1941, and shall supersede the responsibility and authority of the Attorney General under the said Proclamations in respect of such prohibited and restricted areas.

I hereby further authorize and direct the Secretary of War and the said Military Commanders to take such

> "I hereby authorize and direct the Secretary of War . . . to prescribe military areas . . . from which any or all persons may be excluded."

other steps as he or the appropriate Military Commander may deem advisable to enforce compliance with the restrictions applicable to each Military area hereinabove authorized to be designated, including the use of Federal troops and other Federal Agencies, with authority to accept assistance of state and local agencies.

I hereby further authorize and direct all Executive Departments, independent establishments and other Federal Agencies, to assist the Secretary of War or the said Military Commanders in carrying out this Executive Order, including the furnishing of medical aid, hospitalization, food, clothing, transportation, use of land, shelter, and other supplies, equipment, utilities, facilities, and services.

President Franklin D. Roosevelt points to a map while giving a speech about the US entry into World War II. Roosevelt signed Executive Order 9066 allowing military commanders to exclude populations from "military areas" as they saw fit. (**Time & Life Pictures/ Getty Images.**)

This order shall not be construed as modifying or limiting in any way the authority heretofore granted under Executive Order No. 8972 [which gave the Secretary of War and the Secretary of the Navy the ability to take "precautionary" measures for the sake of national defense], dated December 12, 1941, nor shall it be construed as limiting or modifying the duty and responsibility of the Federal Bureau of Investigation, with respect to the investigation of alleged acts of sabotage or the duty and responsibility of the Attorney General and the Department of Justice under the Proclamations of December 7 and 8, 1941, prescribing regulations for the conduct and control of alien enemies, except as such duty and responsibility is superseded by the designation of military areas hereunder.

A Notice of Exclusion for Japanese Americans in San Francisco

John L. DeWitt

Japanese Americans were often notified of their evacuation by notices such as the one transcribed in the following viewpoint. The notices were generally posted in public areas. This one, directed at the "Japanese" in much of the city of San Francisco, was posted on April 1, 1942. It declared that area to be off limits to them as of April 7, 1942. It further notified those to be evacuated where and when they might gather for "further instructions," what they needed to bring with them, and what might happen to any belongings or property they might have to leave behind. When this notice was written, Lieutenant General John L. DeWitt was the chief of the army's Western Defense Command.

SOURCE. John L. DeWitt, "Civilian Exclusion Order No. 5, Western Defense Command and Fourth Army Wartime Civil Control Administration," *Wartime Hysteria: The Role of the Press in the Removal of 110,000 Persons of Japanese Ancestry During World War II*, Japanese American Curriculum Project, April 1, 1942.

Civilian Exclusion Order No. 5
WESTERN DEFENSE COMMAND
AND FOURTH ARMY
WARTIME CIVIL CONTROL ADMINISTRATION
Presidio of San Francisco, California
April 1, 1942

INSTRUCTIONS
TO ALL PERSONS OF
JAPANESE
ANCESTRY
LIVING IN THE FOLLOWING AREA:

All that portion of the City and County of San Francisco, State of California, lying generally west of the north-south line established by Junipero Serra Boulevard, Worcester Avenue, and Nineteenth Avenue, and lying generally north of the east-west line established by California Street, to the intersection of Market Street, and thence on Market Street to San Francisco Bay.

All Japanese persons, both alien and non-alien, will be evacuated from the above designated area by 12:00 o'clock noon, Tuesday, April 7, 1942.

No Japanese person will be permitted to enter or leave the above described area after 8:00 A.M., Thursday, April 2, 1942, without obtaining special permission from the Provost Marshal at the Civil Control Station located at:

1701 Van Ness Avenue
San Francisco, California

The Civil Control Station is equipped to assist the Japanese population affected by this evacuation in the following ways:

1. Give advice and instructions on the evacuation.

2. Provide services with respect to the management, leasing, sale, storage or other disposition of most

kinds of property including: real estate, business and professional equipment, buildings, household goods, boats, automobiles, livestock, etc.

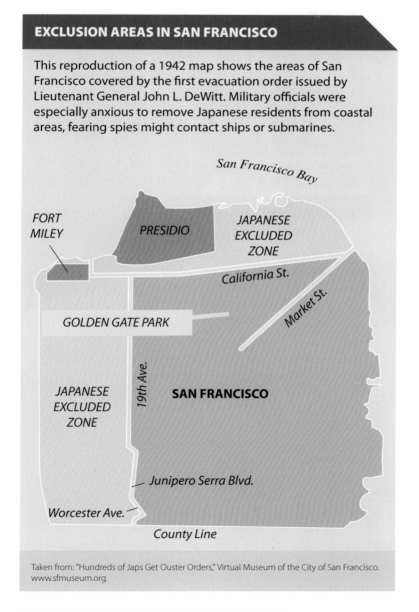

EXCLUSION AREAS IN SAN FRANCISCO

This reproduction of a 1942 map shows the areas of San Francisco covered by the first evacuation order issued by Lieutenant General John L. DeWitt. Military officials were especially anxious to remove Japanese residents from coastal areas, fearing spies might contact ships or submarines.

San Francisco Bay

FORT MILEY

PRESIDIO

JAPANESE EXCLUDED ZONE

California St.

GOLDEN GATE PARK

Market St.

JAPANESE EXCLUDED ZONE

19th Ave.

SAN FRANCISCO

Junipero Serra Blvd.

Worcester Ave.

County Line

Taken from: "Hundreds of Japs Get Ouster Orders," Virtual Museum of the City of San Francisco. www.sfmuseum.org.

3. Provide temporary residence elsewhere for all Japanese in family groups.

4. Transport persons and a limited amount of clothing and equipment to their new residence, as specified below.

THE FOLLOWING INSTRUCTIONS MUST BE OBSERVED:

1. A responsible member of each family, preferably the head of the family, or the person in whose name most of the property is held, and each individual living alone, will report to the Civil Control Station to receive further instructions. This must be done between 8:00 A.M. and 5:00 P.M., Thursday, April 2, 1942, or between 8:00 A.M. and 5:00 P.M., Friday, April 3, 1942.

2. Evacuees must carry with them on departure for the Reception Center, the following property:

(a) Bedding and linens (no mattress) for each member of the family;

(b) Toilet articles for each member of the family;

(c) Extra clothing for each member of the family;

(d) Sufficient knives, forks, spoons, plates, bowls and cups for each member of the family;

(e) Essential personal effects for each member of the family.

All items carried will be securely packaged, tied and plainly marked with the name of the owner and numbered in accordance with instructions received at the Civil Control Station.

The size and number of packages is limited to that which can be carried by the individual or family group.

No contraband items as described in paragraph 6, Public Proclamation No. 3, Headquarters Western Defense Command and Fourth Army, dated March 24, 1942, will be carried.

Photo on previous page: San Francisco area shoppers read a posted sign announcing that all persons of Japanese descent are to be evacuated from the area. (Getty Images.)

3. The United States Government through its agencies will provide for the storage at the sole risk of the owner of the more substantial household items, such as iceboxes, washing machines, pianos and other heavy furniture. Cooking utensils and other small items will be accepted if crated, packed and plainly marked with the name and address of the owner. Only one name and address will be used by a given family.

4. Each family, and individual living alone, will be furnished transportation to the Reception Center. Private means of transportation will not be utilized. All instructions pertaining to the movement will be obtained at the Civil Control Station.

Go to the Civil Control Station at 1701 Van Ness Avenue, San Francisco, California, between 8:00 A.M. and 5:00 P.M., Thursday, April 2, 1942, or between 8:00 A.M. and 5:00 P.M., Friday, April 3, 1942, to receive further instructions.

J. L. DeWITT
Lieutenant General, U. S. Army
Commanding

Life in the Relocation Centers

Caleb Foote

In the following selection, originally published in 1944, a peace activist provides a snapshot of life in the Japanese American internment camps. He describes the living conditions evacuees faced, mentioning the hastily constructed buildings and cheap food. He also notes that those evacuees who worked were paid very little, and all dealt with the psychological implications of having their lives uprooted. The author goes on to suggest that many officials realized that the camps were, at best, an inadequate response to evacuation and, at worst, unfair and unconstitutional. A new emphasis, he writes, was being placed on getting Japanese Americans to settle in parts of the United States outside of the exclusion zone on the Pacific Coast. Indeed, increasing numbers of Japanese Americans were already moving to those areas by 1943. Caleb Foote was a pacifist inspired by the the Quaker religion. He served as a professor of law at the University of Nebraska, the University of Pennsylvania, and the University of California, Berkeley.

SOURCE. Caleb Foote, "Outcasts!—The Story of America's Treatment of Her Japanese American Minority," *The Lost Years 1942–1946*, Moonlight Publications, 1972, pp. 38–43. Content.cdlib.org. Reproduced by permisson.

The Granada Relocation Center at Amache, Colorado, is typical of the ten camps in seven Western states in which evacuated Japanese Americans are living. The centers are managed by a civilian agency, the War Relocation Authority [WRA], appointed by the President for this job. A company of military police is stationed at each center to control entrance and exits. The total cost of maintenance of the evacuees in the centers and administration of the centers is borne by the Federal Government.

The buildings are of a temporary type of construction described as "so very cheap that, frankly, if it stands up for the duration we are going to be lucky." They are grouped in blocks, each composed of twelve residential barracks, a recreation hall (usually used for offices), and two large community buildings containing latrines, laundry, showers, kitchen, and mess hall. Thirty or more such blocks make up a center, usually surrounded by a barbed-wired fence, with military guard towers at intervals.

Residential barracks are 120x20 feet, divided into six one-room apartments, ranging in size from 16x20 to 20x24 feet, with from two to seven people housed in each room. They come equipped only with bed, blankets, and stove. Population at the Granada Center, smallest of the ten, was 7,620 in April, 1943, of whom more than two-thirds are American citizens—born and reared in this country. Most of the 2,123 aliens came here as laborers and merchants in the early 1900's, and have not been allowed to become citizens. About half the population came from rural areas, the other half is urban, and their occupations before evacuation embrace practically every phase of American life.

School children make up one-quarter of the population with 1,909 persons registered from nursery school through high school. Classes taught by both Caucasian and Japanese American teachers are held in barracks

Using whatever materials they could find, parents at the Poston camp in Arizona made toys for their children to play with **(Amber Tiffany/Furuya family, San Diego, CA.)**

with meager equipment. School buildings are now going up at some centers.

Thirty-Eight Cents a Day

Food is served in community mess halls, cafeteria style. Cost of meals for all relocation centers have averaged not more than forty-five cents per person, and there is rationing just as there is outside. Describing the food in one Center, a California newsman wrote: "It is substantial, healthy, and not very appetizing. It is a combination of American and Japanese dishes, and tastes like something bought for about thirty-eight cents a day—which is what it happens to cost. They have no butter, but apparently plenty of margarine, and enough tea to serve it twice a day. Meatless days come at least three times a week."

Employment is offered about half of Granada's population in twenty-five different departments, and the pay ranges from $12.00 to $19.00 a month even for the highest skills, with the government bearing the brunt of maintenance. There are farms at all the centers, employing many people. This typical relocation center had a 150-bed hospital, a biweekly newspaper, fire and police departments, and an elected community council to handle minor governmental functions. Cooperative stores, with 2,387 members, gross more than $40,000.00 per month.

Paternalistic Democracies

Set up to receive people evacuated from Pacific Coast areas, the ten relocation centers were to have been self-supporting paternalistic democracies. As nearly half of the evacuees of working age had agricultural experience, it was hoped that they could raise all their own food and a surplus as well, with some industries thrown in to make the communities as self-sufficient as possible.

> A camp in which one racial group is segregated is an un-American and unhealthy thing.

Plans were formulated for limited self-government, for schools under advanced education methods, for stores cooperatively operated by and for the community. In short, far-sighted War Relocation Authority policy sought to undo as much of the harm caused by the evacuation as possible.

Actual practice has fallen short of these ideals. The inhospitable locations of the relocation centers, the low wage scale, the rising demand for resettlement outside the centers, the pressures against the WRA, and deep psychological factors have all worked to modify original plans and ideals. It is now realized that no matter how well planned and administered, a camp in which one racial group is segregated is an un-American and unhealthy thing. Thus the WRA is now bending its policy toward resettlement outside the centers.

Inhospitable Landscapes

The location of the centers alone has been enough to deny any possibility that they might speedily become self-supporting. The Hearst columnist who in the early days of the war wanted these people moved into the interior—"and I don't mean a nice part of the interior, either"—certainly got his wish. At Poston, Arizona, site of the largest center (Population 20,000), the three sections of the camp were nicknamed Roaston, Toaston, and Duston, and the names tell the truth about most of the centers, where desert heat and dust are bywords in summer. The camps have the hardships of the typical frontier community—mud, inadequate housing, physical hardship, and subjugation of desert land, but without the zest and self-interest of voluntary pioneering.

Factors beyond [the] control of the War Relocation Authority probably forced these locations, for a center had to be away from military zones but near adequate transportation and power, had to have agricultural possibilities on land owned or controlled by the government (to prevent speculation), but could not displace already existing white settlers. Coupled with these restrictions was vigorous local opposition wherever the War Relocation Authority went. Typical of the ignorant prejudice of every Western state was Idaho Governor [Chase] Clark's statement: "Japs live like rats, breed like rats, and act like rats. We don't want them buying or leasing land and becoming permanently located in our state." The result was that with limited exceptions the relocation centers were established where nobody else wanted to live: Western desert, arid Great Plains or cut-over parts of Arkansas.

Resentment at the low wage scales is another factor that has disrupted relocation center life. The evacuees employed at the centers receive $19.00 a month for

TYPICAL BARRACKS BLOCKS AT JAPANESE AMERICAN INTERNMENT CAMPS

Poston Manzanar   Gila River   Tule Lake   Tule Lake (later)

Granada, Heart Mountain, Jerome, Rowher, Topaz   Minidoka

Barracks		Mess hall
Ironing room		Recreation bldg.
Laundry		Storage room
Men's latrine		Women's latrine

Taken from: Jeffrey F. Burton, Mary M. Farrell, Florence B. Lord, and Richard W. Lord, *Confinement and Ethnicity: An Overview of World War II Japanese American Relocation Sites*. National Park Service, 1999.

skilled or professional labor, $12.00 for "apprentices," with the great majority getting $16.00 a month. In addition, all those in the centers receive meals costing not over forty-five cents a day and minimum housing. It is natural that American citizens and aliens convicted of no crime should resent such sub-standard pay. This feeling is accentuated because Caucasians working within the Centers receive standard pay. Thus many white school teachers receive in the neighborhood of $2,000.00 a year, but an accredited Japanese American teacher doing the same job, will get but $19.00 a month. These low wage scales mean that many families are using up their reserves and that many others face destitution. The drabness of much of the work, coupled with these small allowances, offers no individual incentive, and many persons find time hanging heavily on their hands.

> "Evacuation has created or accentuated psychological and mental attitudes that do far more harm than physical suffering or hardship.

In the early days of detention, a little girl saw a dog trying to climb through the barbed-wire fence into an Assembly Center. "Don't come in here, little dog," she cried. "You won't be able to go back to America." That thought more than anything else explains the failure of the relocation center as a way of life. Evacuation has created or accentuated psychological and mental attitudes that do far more harm than physical suffering or hardship.

A Suffering That Spans Generations

Evacuation effectively smashed the hopes and dreams of both old and young. The older, alien Japanese, although themselves denied the right to become American citizens, have helped build America and have sacrificed their lives so that their children might enjoy the fruits of American citizenship. Evacuation has meant for them a bitter realization of failure. The discrimination against their children has caused them intense suffering; and for themselves separated from the homes and jobs of a lifetime, they know they are too old to start again.

For the younger American citizens of Japanese ancestry the disappointment has been as sharp. As Rep. Clifton A. Woodrum of Virginia observed, "there has been a terrific dislocation for those who are American citizens. They were picked up body and baggage and moved out, and I imagine it would have a severe psychological effect upon a man who was really a loyal American citizen."

The insecurity of not knowing what will happen next is the most pronounced characteristic of both aliens and citizens in the relocation centers. Property losses before and during the evacuation, the sense of constantly being pushed about, change of official policy, government promises freely given and freely broken—all these have bred a fear and cynicism that bodes no good for the future. There is ample basis for this insecurity. A young American-born farmer who lived on the California coast was urged by the Army to move voluntarily out of the zone that was to be evacuated. He moved to an inland part of the State, bought a farm, put in his crops, and sent for his family. Then the Army changed its mind, the remaining part of California was frozen, and he was evacuated. Many thousands like this young man moved in accordance with requests only to be caught by later changes of policy.

Cost Is Too High

The cost in money and manpower has been high. The first year of evacuation cost some $210,000,000, plus the services of many soldiers and thousands of workers, including skilled administrators, needed elsewhere in a time of manpower shortage. In addition, close to 50,000 of those evacuated had been employed at useful labor, nearly half of them in agriculture, where they are so desperately needed today.

Future Courses of Action

Two courses are open. One is to continue and expand the individual resettlement program already started, with the end of getting all those who are loyal out of the relocation centers and back into American life. It would involve eventual return of some of the people to the Pacific Coast as soon as the military considers that safe, but for economic reasons most of the people probably will not return to the Coast. Such a resettlement policy, coupled with adequate government protection and the economic means

> A resettlement policy, coupled with adequate government protection and the economic means to start life again, would be a fair and sensible solution.

to start life again, would be a fair and sensible solution to the problem. The net result would be the distribution of this tiny minority of one-tenth of one percent of our population throughout the country, where re-absorption into American life would be rapidly completed.

The alternative is seen in the vigorous anti-Japanese campaign now in full swing in California and its repercussions, which are being felt throughout the country. This movement has three objectives: (1) to return control of Japanese Americans from the WRA to the Army, apparently with the hope that Americans of Japanese parentage can then be used as forced labor gangs at low cost; (2) to deprive American citizens of Japanese ancestry of their citizenship; (3) to prevent Japanese Americans from re-entering California.

The consequences for success for this anti-Japanese American effort for those people would be catastrophic both for the Japanese Americans and for Americans generally. Former Governor [Ralph] Carr of Colorado has accurately described the situation in these words:

> If we do not extend humanity's kindness and understanding to these people (evacuees), if we deny them

the protection of the Bill of Rights, if we say they may be denied the privilege of living in any of the forty-eight states, and force them into concentration camps without hearing or charge of misconduct, then we are tearing down the whole American system. If these people are not to be accorded all the rights and privileges which the Constitution gives them, then those same rights and privileges may be denied to you and me six months from now for another just as poor reason as the one which is now offered against the Japanese.

After a Long Struggle, Survivors of the Camps Received Official Redress

Japanese American National Museum

The following selection examines the process by which Japanese Americans who had been sent to World War II internment camps finally achieved an official apology as well as the promise of financial compensation from the US government. The process began in the 1960s and 1970s and was often led by activist Sansei, or third-generation Japanese Americans who were born either in the camps or after World War II. Taking advantage of the broader movement advocating the expansion of civil rights in those decades, activists worked with both Japanese American groups and government officials. Some of those who played a major part in moving the effort forward were Japanese Americans serving in the US Congress. Some Japanese Americans, including some community leaders, disagreed with the calls for redress. But, as the authors of the selection indicate, the struggle resulted in the founding of a

Commission on Wartime Relocation and Internment of Civilians in 1980. The commission's work led to the Civil Liberties Act of 1988, which was signed into law by President Ronald Reagan.

For Japanese American organizations and civil rights institutions across the country, 2008 is a very important year because it marks the twentieth anniversary of the Civil Liberties Act of 1988. Signed into law by President Ronald Reagan on August 10, 1988, this legislation provided an apology and compensation to the thousands of Japanese Americans whose constitutional rights were violated during their World War II forced exclusion and mass incarceration.

Between 1942 and 1945, thousands of Japanese Americans were forcibly removed from their homes on the West Coast and parts of Hawai'i and approximately 120,000 were detained in concentration camps or Department of Justice camps built in some of the country's harshest, most undesirable landscapes. This was a deeply traumatic experience for the Japanese American community. Some communities had as little as 48 hours notice to prepare for their removal, causing many Japanese American families to suffer enormous monetary losses by having to abandon or sell businesses, homes, and belongings at far below market value. Other families carried deep emotional scars from the shame of being marked as disloyal, from the upheavals of exclusion and incarceration, and from the pressures of having to rebuild their lives after the end of World War II.

After Internment

The decades following World War II marked a period when members of the Japanese American community worked hard to re-establish businesses and careers—some from scratch—and to regain a sense of normalcy in their lives. Having just endured the stigma and humiliation of incarceration, most Japanese Americans sought to keep a low profile and avoid being singled out again. This was also understandable given the high levels of anti-Japanese sentiment that persisted after the war. Therefore, the country remained silent when it came to the issue of providing redress and reparations to Japanese Americans for the gross violation of their constitutional rights during incarceration.

The Civil Rights Movement of the 1960s ushered a significant change in the nation's political climate when it came to combating racial discrimination and acknowledging the rights of minorities. The 1960s and 1970s also marked the coming of age for the Sansei (third-generation Japanese Americans), many of who were born during or after incarceration, and therefore too young to have experienced its worst ordeals.

> Sansei and younger Nisei . . . mobilized efforts to seek a formal apology and compensation from the federal government.

A New Generation

Starting in the late 1960s and early 1970s, Sansei and younger Nisei (second-generation Japanese Americans) mobilized efforts to seek a formal apology and compensation from the federal government for their unjust actions during World War II. This turned out to be far from easy however, for several reasons. First, they were working against precedence in compelling the government to formally acknowledge past wrongs and provide redress, not to mention the possibility of forcing Americans to confront past inequities against other groups. Second, they faced opposition from outspoken critics who either did not believe in the necessity of reparations or denounced the incarceration experience as falsehood, not to mention politicians and judges who did not believe in redress. Even the Japanese American community stood

President Ronald Reagan (seated) signed the Civil Liberties Act of 1988 into law on August 10, officially apologizing to and monetarily compensating Japanese Americans for the forced internments during World War II. (Associated Press.)

divided on the issue, with some calling for restitution and others opposing the effort for a variety of reasons (i.e., feelings that any form of reparations and assignation of monetary value would trivialize the sufferings of the experience, fears of racist backlash, apprehension that any redress efforts could succeed). Third, even those in agreement of pursuing redress harbored different ideas of how they should proceed.

Seeking Avenues for Redress

Eventually, the proponents of redress divided into two main groups. The first favored seeking redress through the legislative branch, while the second felt that redress should be sought through the judiciary. The group in favor of legislation was led by the Japanese American Citizens' League (JACL), which stood as the Japanese American organization with the most political clout. One of the most important steps that the JACL took was to arrange a meeting in 1979 with Senator Daniel Inouye, Senator Spark Matsunaga, Congressman Norman Mineta, and Congressman Robert Matsui, the four Japanese American members of the U.S. Congress at the time besides Senator S.I. Hayakawa, who was not invited because of his known opposition to redress. Having their support would be crucial if the effort to obtain redress from the legislature was to succeed. During this meeting, all four members of Congress agreed that seeking redress was important and affirmed their desire to help achieve the goal. However, Senator Inouye suggested that it would be better to form a congressional commission to investigate the government's wartime actions and recommend any actions that should be taken to address any damages. Although this additional step would push back the redress timeline—then a daunting prospect, given that former inmates were passing away at a rapid rate—Senator Inouye argued that it was a necessary one in ultimately convincing the government and the public of the validity of the redress cause. As a result, members of the JACL agreed to proceed according to Senator Inouye's recommendation, instead of pushing for a redress bill right away.

Meanwhile, another group was spearheaded by William Hohri of Chicago, who launched the National Council for Japanese American Redress (NCJAR) in 1979. Hohri disagreed with JACL's decision to lobby for a study commission and felt that the best way to seek redress was through the federal court system. As a result, he filed a class-action lawsuit containing 22 causes of action against the federal government in May 1983 on behalf of 25 Japanese American plaintiffs and the NCJAR. In all, the lawsuit sought $27 billion in damages ($10,000 per internee). NCJAR promoted awareness on the redress issue and mobilized the Japanese American community which contributed to the successful drive for congressional action. A third group, the National Coalition for Redress/Reparations, also formed at the same time, seeking to pursue redress by lobbying Congress directly.

> "The Civil Liberties Act acknowledged the federal government's wrongdoings against Japanese Americans during World War II through a formal apology."

With Senators Inouye and Matsunaga leading the way, a bipartisan group of senators introduced the Commission on Wartime Relocation and Internment of Civilians Act (CWRIC) that President Jimmy Carter would sign into law on July 31, 1980. This bipartisan commission consisted of distinguished figures from diverse backgrounds set out to conduct a series of hearings from July to December 1981. NCJAR and JACL were instrumental in recruiting and preparing individuals to speak at the hearings. In all, CWRIC called over 750 witnesses from throughout the country to testify about their wartime incarceration. Ultimately, these hearings would not only convince CWRIC that gross constitutional violations had been committed and that redress was necessary, [but] they also served as an important cathartic experience for many former inmates who had kept silent about their wartime experience for decades. CWRIC would release a 467-page report in 1983 recommending the federal government to issue a national apology, compensate each surviving eligible individual $20,000, and set up an educational and humanitarian foundation, among other measures. Hindsight would show that the establishment of CWRIC and its public hearings was critical in paving the way for redress legislation and bolstering its credibility.

The American Guarantee of Birthright Citizenship

Perhaps the most controversial aspect of Japanese American internment during World War II was the fact that many of those sent to relocation camps were US citizens rather than resident aliens or recent immigrants. The US Constitution grants certain rights to all citizens, including the right to not be detained without due cause (such as suspicion of illegal activities) and the due process of law (such as a formal accusation of crimes and then conviction in a legitimate trial). Therefore those Japanese Americans who enjoyed US citizenship felt strongly that their rights as citizens were being denied them.

When the United States was first formed in the late 1700s, the right of citizenship was limited to "free white persons." These included both people who were born on US soil and immigrants who followed established naturalization procedures. Those who were not "free white persons" included the millions of slaves of African descent, a small population of free blacks, and Native Americans, who were commonly considered citizens of their own tribal "nations." Free blacks enjoyed rights that varied from state to state, but they generally were banned from exercising such rights as voting or sitting on juries. However, the US Supreme Court's infamous *Dred Scott* decision in 1857 claimed that people of African descent, whether free or slave, could not be citizens by virtue of their race.

The *Dred Scott* decision was overturned by a clause in the 14th Amzendment to the US Constitution. This amendment, ratified in 1868 after the Civil War and the freeing of slaves, affirmed that "all persons born or naturalized in the United States, and subjection to the jurisdiction thereof, are citizens of the United States." In other words, the right of US citizenship is granted simply by being born on American soil. Although it continues to be controversial, the principle of "birthright citizenship" has survived many legal challenges since 1868.

Presidential Signatures

After a series of votes in Congress, the Senate and the House of Representatives both passed legislation to accept the findings of the CWRIC Report and implement redress measures. The bill on redress was finally signed into law by Ronald Reagan on August 10, 1988, and named the Civil Liberties Act of 1988. The Civil Liberties Act acknowledged the federal government's wrongdoings against Japanese Americans during World War II through a formal apology. In addition, the act also appropriated over a billion dollars in compensation to be paid to each surviving internee ($20,000 per individual), as well as an educational trust fund to promote awareness of the World War II internment and prevent similar injustices from recurring in the future.

Ultimately, the success of redress was attributed to several factors, including changes to the nation's political climate, mobilization efforts from the Japanese American community, and the actions of key Japanese American politicians, organizations, and individuals. Today, many organizations and communities continue to commemorate the experiences of World War II and subsequent victory in redress around February 19 of each year, also known as the Day of Remembrance. This marks the date in 1942 when President [Franklin] Roosevelt signed Executive Order 9066, which led to the unconstitutional exclusion of Japanese Americans. Observing this important day helps serve as a reminder of past injustices against civil rights, and that we must continue to take action and speak out against constitutional violations whenever they occur.

Some Survivors of the Camps Seek to Preserve Them as Memorials

Justin Ewers

In recent years, as the following selection notes, some Japanese Americans have taken steps to turn the World War II-era internment camps into official memorials. The author writes that very little remains of most of the camps, but former internees and historical preservationists hope that parts of them might not only be preserved but reconstructed, and that special informational centers will be built. The model has been established by the Manzanar camp in the deserts of Southern California, which was the first to be named a national historic site in 1992. The key problem, the author reports, appears to be the funding of such memorials. Journalist Justin Ewers writes for *U.S. News & World Report*.

SOURCE. Justin Ewers, "Former Japanese American Internees Fight to Preserve Internment Camps," *World War II*, vol. 23.3, August–September 2008. Copyright © 2008 by Weider History Group. Reproduced by permission of Weider History Group.

Betty Abe was fifteen years old when she heard the news, playing with her sisters in the cantaloupe crates on her family's farm outside Los Angeles. "My dad had predicted maybe six months before that war was going to start," remembers Abe, now eighty-two. On the morning of December 7, 1941, her family's worst fears were realized. She and her sisters climbed out of the crates, went into their house, and asked the same question on the minds of many Americans: "What is Pearl Harbor?"

For Abe, whose parents hailed from Japan, playtime was over. In her community, and elsewhere on the West Coast, Japanese Americans were accused of disloyalty. The following summer the government turned on them, too, shipping nearly one hundred twenty thousand people, most of them born in the United States, to ten internment camps scattered across the West. Betty Abe would spend the rest of her high school years living behind barbed wire.

When the war ended, the Abes, like the rest of the internees, were told to leave the camps. The camps themselves—small cities of tarpaper barracks and wooden mess halls—were dismantled. By 1947, they had nearly vanished.

Only recently have former internees begun making a concerted effort to preserve not just their stories of internment, but the camps themselves. In 1992, Manzanar—the camp in southern California that housed the Abe family—became the first to be named a national historic site. Several others have been given honorary designations as national historic landmarks. In 2006, President [George W.] Bush signed a bill authorizing up to $38 million for a new grant program devoted to the camps' preservation, the first federal effort to preserve the entire camp system. Two years later, though, the funds have yet to be appropriated.

Local groups around each of the camps, meanwhile, are fighting to protect what's left. At most of them, a few

Photo on following page: In 1992, the Manzanar War Relocation Center, where this monument stands, became the first World War II internment camp to be named a national historic site. (Getty Images.)

> 'It takes a while for people to figure out these [internment sites] are historic, which is a shame.'

outbuildings and concrete foundations are all that remain. "It takes a while for people to figure out these places are historic, which is a shame," says Jeff Burton, a park service archaeologist who began studying the camps in the 1990s.

The few relics that have survived the last sixty years include, remarkably, the jail at Tule Lake, a camp in northern California where internees considered disloyal were sent. Pat Shiono, who chairs the camp's preservation committee, has been visiting the site (much of which is now used as a highway maintenance yard) for more than a decade. "We've been going there every year watching the jail sort of melting away," she says. The building has been vandalized; rain and wind have worn it down. "It was an abandoned shack and I don't think anybody understood what it was," she says. "We keep thinking, 'Oh my God, in another ten to twenty years, it won't be here.'" Working with the state transportation agency that owns the land, Shiono's group recently had a fence built around the jail and a shelter put over it.

Not Much Money for Preservation

Other camps, too, are beginning to emerge from years of neglect. In the 1990s, a preservation group near Heart Mountain War Relocation Center in Wyoming was able to restore the camp's "honor roll," a large panel in the center of the site that includes the name of every person in the camp who served in the military during the war. At the Topaz internment camp in Utah, which sat on nineteen thousand acres during World War II, a preservation committee has raised enough funds to buy up more than six hundred acres of the site. The group is trying to raise $3.5 million to build an interpretive center there as well. "It's not huge money, but it's huge for us," says Jane Beckwith, the group's president. Beckwith recognizes that she and her fellow preservationists face an uphill battle: not only are the camps on forgotten land far from urban centers, but they don't represent one of the country's prouder moments. "This isn't very happy history," says Beckwith. "I've often thought some night I should go out and plant some dinosaur footprints, then unearth them the next day. I think we'd have money much more quickly."

"I think it's a good idea for people to [preserve the camps] now," Betty Abe says, while she and other internees are still able to contribute. When her family was told to leave the camps in 1945, the authorities handed each internee $25 and a one-way ticket to anywhere in the country. The camps—what's left of them—will require more help than that.

CHAPTER 2

Controversies Over Japanese American Internment

Internment of Japanese Americans Is Necessary and Justified

San Francisco News

The following selection is an editorial printed in a San Francisco newspaper on March 6, 1942, just as plans to require Japanese Americans to evacuate the West Coast were taking shape. It makes arguments typical of other newspapers of the day in asserting that, while unfortunate, the evacuation is the best solution to what seem to be imminent threats. These include the possibility of Japanese Americans committing sabotage or espionage in the "combat zone" along the West Coast, and the chance of attacks on Japanese Americans themselves by angry Caucasian citizens. The editorial's authors also assert that the plans for evacuation and relocation themselves are quite reasonable, and that cooperation on the part of the evacuees is the best way to prove their loyalty.

Photo on previous page: A couple returns to the Manzanar internment camp where they were required to live many decades before. **(Getty Images.)**

SOURCE. *San Francisco News*, "Their Best Way to Show Loyalty," March 6, 1942. Reproduced by permission.

Japanese leaders in California who are counseling their people, both aliens and native-born, to cooperate with the Army in carrying out the evacuation plans are, in effect, offering the best possible way for all Japanese to demonstrate their loyalty to the United States.

Many aliens [Japanese Americans born overseas] and practically all the native-born have been protesting their allegiance to this Government. Although their removal to inland districts outside the military zones may inconvenience them somewhat, even work serious hardships upon some, they must certainly recognize the necessity of clearing the coastal combat areas of all possible fifth columnists [spies] and saboteurs. Inasmuch as the presence of enemy agents cannot be detected readily when these areas are thronged by Japanese, the only course left is to remove all persons of that race for the duration of the war.

That is a clear-cut policy easily understood. Its execution should be supported by all citizens of whatever racial background, but especially it presents an opportunity to the people of an enemy race to prove their spirit of co-operation and keep their relations with the rest of the population of this country on the firm ground of friendship.

> "The most humane way . . . is to move the Japanese out of harm's way and make it as easy as possible for them to go and to remain away until the war is over."

Every indication has been given that the transfer will be made with the least possible hardship. General [John L.] DeWitt's order [of evacuation] was issued in such a way as to give those who can make private moving arrangements plenty of time to do so. All others will not be moved until arrangements can be made for places for them to go. They may have to be housed in temporary quarters until permanent ones can be provided for them, but during the

The Detention of German and Italian Americans

The United States' enemies during World War II included Germany and Italy, as well as Japan. Some members of German or Italian communities faced the threat of detention during the war, but the US government never threatened large-scale relocation for these groups. Altogether, some 11,000 German Americans were detained along with approximately 450 Italian Americans. The larger number of German Americans is partly explained by the fact that many of those interned for suspicion lived with their families in the relocation camps, generally in the southern United States. Those of German or Italian descent who enjoyed US citizenship were not threatened unless a strong case could be made of anti-American activity, such as espionage.

Germany had, since the mid-1800s, supplied large numbers of immigrants to the United States, and even by the 1940s there were so many recent arrivals from that country that wholesale detention was considered virtually impossible. Most of those who were eventually detained were German Americans who were not US citizens, either by birth or by the process of naturalization. Although the military considered asking for the evacuation of these German Americans from military zones on both the Pacific and Atlantic coasts, those plans were abandoned in favor of considering each case individually. German Americans who maintained extensive ties to their homeland or who had been active in pro-Nazi organizations in the United States were the prominent targets.

There were far more Italian residents potentially subject to detention than either Japanese or Germans. Between 1880 and 1924, millions of Italians had immigrated to the United States, and more than 600,000 of them were still not naturalized citizens in 1941. Regulations required that such noncitizens be deemed "enemy aliens" and subject to official registration. While relatively few were sent to detention camps, nearly 10,000 Italian Americans were forced to move inland, away from the military zones on the coasts. Some Italian Americans were also prevented from holding "sensitive" jobs such as deep-sea fishing or working in ports.

A group of people of Japanese descent board a bus for Manzanar, an internment camp in the California desert. Many Americans felt that the relocations, while unfortunate, were the best way to guard against Japanese spies during World War II. (Getty Images.)

summer months that does not mean they will be unduly uncomfortable.

Their property will be carefully protected by the Federal Government, their food and shelter will be provided to the extent they are not able to provide it for themselves, and they will be furnished plenty of entertainment and recreation. That is not according to the pattern of the European concentration camp by any means.

Real danger would exist for all Japanese if they remained in the combat area. The least act of sabotage might provoke angry reprisals that easily could balloon into bloody race riots.

We must avoid any chance of that sort of thing. The most sensible, the most humane way to insure against it is to move the Japanese out of harm's way and make it as easy as possible for them to go and to remain away until the war is over.

Blame-shifting and Wartime Hysteria Led to the Relocation of Japanese Americans

Roger Daniels

The decision to order Japanese Americans to evacuate the West Coast of the United States evolved over a period of weeks during the winter of 1941–42. According to historian Roger Daniels, the decision was the result of a simmering anti-Japanese hysteria that reached its height immediately following the Japanese Navy's attack on Pearl Harbor on December 7, 1941. In the aftermath of the attack, high-ranking US officials looked for someone to blame and hit upon Japanese Americans, first in Hawaii itself. Meanwhile, rumors of Japanese naval attacks on the West Coast stirred up even greater hysteria reflected in major newspapers and in the actions of nervous military men. For Daniels, this sort of scapegoating and hysteria had little basis in fact. He argues that ordinary security forces, such as the FBI, could have easily handled any possible sabotage. Roger Daniels was a professor of history at the University of Cincinnati. His books include *Coming to America* and *Not Like Us: Immigrants and Minorities in America, 1890–1924.*

L eft to their own devices, the internal security forces would have allowed most Japanese Americans to continue with their lives. There would have been special stress for people with a Japanese face—the face of the enemy—but most of them could have coped. But internal security was not left to the specialists: the press, the public, politicians, and some military officials began to clamor that something had to be done about the "Japs who were running around loose." This clamor was effective, in the final analysis, because, from the White House down, there was a "failure of political leadership," as the Commission on the Wartime Relocation and Internment of Civilians noted four decades later. Once anti-Japanese public and political opinion began to prevail, the internal security forces, particularly the FBI and its head, J. Edgar Hoover, joined the chorus. A contributing factor was the string of humiliating defeats that the United States and its allies suffered in the first six months of the war as Japanese imperial forces "ran wild," overrunning Hong Kong, Wake Island, the Philippines, and most of the rest of Southeast Asia, and threatening India and Australia.

In addition, the devastating defeat that [Japanese admiral Isoroku] Yamamoto's strike force inflicted on the United States Navy made some of those in positions of responsibility anxious to blame someone else for their own ineptitude. The worst example of this was Secretary of the Navy Frank Knox's deliberate lying. Returning from a quick inspection of the damage at Pearl Harbor, the full scope of which was still classified, the former

Chicago newspaper publisher blamed "treachery" and "the most effective fifth column [espionage] work that's come out of this war, except in Norway." Knox didn't have to mention Japanese Americans by name. He knew that it was not treachery but incompetence that had allowed the Imperial Japanese Navy to strike such an effective blow. (Orders for the dismissal of Admiral Husband E. Kimmel, the naval commander in Hawaii, were already in the works.) Four days later, in a December 19 [1941] cabinet meeting at the White House, it was decided that all alien Japanese in Hawaii should be interned. This was the first post-Pearl Harbor decision about Japanese Americans to be taken at the highest levels of government, but it was never implemented.

Some of this national hysteria actually preceded Pearl Harbor. One congressman, John D. Dingell (D-Mich.), father of the present Congressman Dingell [John, Jr.], wrote President [Franklin] Roosevelt on August 18, 1941, at a time when the Japanese government was making it difficult for about a hundred Americans to leave Japan, to suggest that the United States should "cause the forceful . . . imprisonment in a concentration camp of ten thousand alien Japanese in Hawaii." The Japanese attack, coming without warning and while special Japanese envoys were negotiating in Washington, set off a stream of venom, and the cry of treachery, directed at anything Japanese. On the day after Pearl Harbor the Los Angeles *Times*, the most important paper in Southern California, announced that California was "a zone of danger" and noted:

> The day after Pearl Harbor the Los Angeles *Times* . . . announced that California was 'a zone of danger.'

> We have thousands of Japanese here . . . Some, perhaps many . . . are good Americans. What the rest may be we do not know, nor can we take a chance in the light of

yesterday's demonstration that treachery and double-dealing are major Japanese weapons.

The *Times*, which used the word "Japanese," was more polite than many West Coast papers, which habitually said "Japs" and often used terms such as "Nips," "mad dogs," and "yellow vermin." It was not just regional journalists who whipped up hysteria. Two days after Pearl Harbor, the nationally syndicated columnist Westbrook Pegler proposed that the United States adopt the methods of its enemies. For every hostage the Axis murdered, he wrote, the United States should retaliate by killing "100 victims selected out of [American] concentration camps," which Pegler assumed would be set up for subversive Germans and Italians and "alien Japanese."

Throughout the winter and into the spring, until Japanese Americans were cooped up in concentration camps, a barrage of stories stressing the presumed threat of Japanese Americans to the safety of the nation filled the press and the airwaves. The following headlines, chiefly about imaginary events, ran in the Los Angeles *Times* between December 8, 1941, and February 23, 1942:

> *Until Japanese Americans were cooped up in concentration camps, a barrage of stories stressing the presumed threat . . . to the safety of the nation filled the press and the airwaves.*

JAP BOAT FLASHES MESSAGE ASHORE
ENEMY PLANES SIGHTED OVER
CALIFORNIA COAST
TWO JAPS WITH MAPS AND ALIEN
LITERATURE SEIZED
JAP AND CAMERA HELD IN BAY CITY
CAPS ON JAPANESE TOMATO PLANTS POINT
TO AIR BASE
JAPANESE HERE SENT VITAL DATA TO TOKYO
CHINESE ABLE TO SPOT JAP

MAP REVEALS JAP MENACE
Network of Alien Farms Covers Strategic Defense
Areas over Southland
JAPS PLAN ATTACK IN APRIL WARNS CHIEF
OF KOREAN SPY BAND

Much of this jingoism was disseminated by the West Coast military authorities, including some who quickly regretted it. Major General Joseph W. Stilwell, not yet the famous "Vinegar Joe" of Burma fame, but already possessed of a tart tongue, was, in December 1941, the corps commander responsible for defending Southern California. He recorded in his shirt-pocket diary his day-to-day reactions, including the following:

DEC. 8—Sunday night "air raid" at San Francisco . . . Fourth Army kind of jittery.

DEC. 9—. . . Fleet of thirty-four [Japanese] ships between San Francisco and Los Angeles. Later—not authentic.

DEC. 11—[Phone call from 4th Army] "The main Japanese fleet is 164 miles off San Francisco." I believed it, like a damn fool . . . Of course [4th Army] passed the buck on this report. They had it from a "usually reliable source," but they should never have put it out without check.

DEC. 13—Not content with the above blah, [4th] Army pulled another at ten-thirty today. "Reliable information that attack on Los Angeles is imminent. A general alarm being considered . . ." What jackass would send a general alarm [which would have called for the evacuation of Los Angeles] under the circumstances. The [4th] Army G-2 [Intelligence] is just another amateur, just like all the rest of the staff. Rule: the higher the headquarters, the more important is *calm*.

Photo on previous page: US Secretary of the Navy Frank Knox stoked the flames of anti-Japanese sentiment by blaming the Japanese surprise attack on Pearl Harbor, Hawaii, on spies and "treachery" rather than the navy's incompetence. **(Getty Images.)**

A Politician Claims the Internment Camps Were Justifiable

Photo on follow-
ing page: The USS
California was one of
several ships lost in
the surprise attack on
Pearl Harbor, Hawaii, by
the Japanese Navy Air
Force. US assemblyman
Gil Ferguson asserted
that the internments
during World War II
were justified in light
of the destruction and
American lives lost
in the attack. **(Getty
Images.)**

Katherine Bishop

In the following selection, *New York Times* reporter Katherine
Bishop writes of a rare voice trying to claim, forty years after the
fact, that the internment camps were justified. This opinion was
voiced by California state legislator Gil Ferguson, who asserted
that the camps were the product of military necessity and introduced a bill into the State Assembly to recognize this. Ferguson
also objected to any attempt to refer to the internment camps as
"concentration camps" as, he claimed, they were nothing like the
notorious camps maintained by Nazi Germany or Imperial Japan
during the war years. Ferguson's proposed bill was rejected by
committees both times it was introduced, failing to even achieve
an assembly-wide vote.

SOURCE. Katherine Bishop, "Bill on Internees Raises New Alarm,"
New York Times, August 28, 1990. Reproduced by permission.

A state legislator has raised concerns among Japanese-Americans in California by proposing a resolution to revise what schoolchildren are taught about the internment of Japanese-Americans during World War II.

The legislator, Assemblyman Gil Ferguson, a Republican from Orange County, seeks to have children taught that Japanese-Americans were not interned in "concentation camps," but rather were held in relocation centers justified by military necessity.

The State Assembly will vote on the measure on Tuesday [August 28, 1990]. Mr. Ferguson, who said he acted at the request of two groups, the Survivors of Pearl Harbor and Survivors of Bataan, conceded that it has little chance. If the resolution fails Tuesday, he said, he will try to revive it by getting support from other veterans' groups.

Countering a Resolution

The resolution is intended to counter a measure passed last year urging that children here be taught that there was no military basis for the internment, and that it resulted primarily from "race prejudice."

In the internment, which was ordered by President Franklin D. Roosevelt, more than 110,000 Americans of Japanese ancestry, many of them American citizens, were held against their will from 1942 until 1946.

Mr. Ferguson said he particularly objected to references to the internment camps and relocation centers as "concentration camps."

"Concentration camps are those like the Germans had or those in China run by the Japanese where people were starved, experimented on, injected with germs and killed," he said. "I take strong objection, and

> 'Concentration camps are those like the Germans had or those in China run by the Japanese where people were starved, experimented on, injected with germs and killed.'

I'm repulsed by anyone who says we had those. I'm not going to let these liberals rewrite history."

Looking Back in Sorrow

In recent years, a number of actions have been taken to address what has come to be viewed by many as a massive violation of the civil rights of those of Japanese ancestry who were living in this country at the outbreak of the war.

The Federal Commission on Wartime Relocation and Internment of Civilians, which was created by President Jimmy Carter in 1980 to study the issue, concluded that the internment was not justified by military necessity. It listed the "historical causes" shaping the decision to relocate Japanese-Americans to be "race prejudice, war hysteria and a failure of political leadership."

> The 'concentration camp' issue was 'a matter of semantics.'

The Supreme Court, in its 1944 decision in *Korematsu v. United States*, upheld the constitutionality of the relocation program. But in the early 1980's, those whose arrests for failure to comply with relocation orders had led to the Supreme Court cases brought new appeals of their convictions. The conviction of Fred Korematsu was overturned in Federal district Court here in November 1983.

"Contradicts the Facts"

Michael Iwahiro, president of the Sacramento chapter of the Japanese American Citizens League, which is opposing Mr. Ferguson's resolution, said it was "factually inaccurate and contradicts the facts supported by the Federal Commission."

Mr. Iwahiro said the "concentration camp" issue was "a matter of semantics."

"There was barbed wire and military police, and people could not freely come and go," he said of the internment camps.

About 77,000 of those affected by the order were American citizens. Mr. Ferguson said today that the Government had the right under international law to declare those who were not citizens to be enemy aliens following the attack on Pearl Harbor and the United States' declaration of war. He said that the small children of these aliens who were American citizens by virtue of being born in this country were interned with them "only because their fathers insisted they come with them."

Seen as "Ill-Conceived"

Should the measure pass the floor vote of the Assembly, it would go to the Senate for a vote this week.

Dale Minami, one of the lawyers who worked to overturn the convictions in the internment cases, today called the measure "tremendously ill-conceived."

He said that many Americans of Japanese ancestry are concerned that the resolution is "a prelude to an attempt to reverse the redress bill in 1991, which is the 50th anniversary of Pearl Harbor."

In the redress bill, known as the Civil Liberties Act of 1988, Congress pledged restitution of $20,000 to each of the surviving 60,000 Americans of Japanese descent who were relocated. The money is meant to compensate former detainees for lost freedom, jobs and belongings.

The oldest surviving detainees are to be compensated first. According to William J. Yoshino, the national director of the Japanese American Citizens League, payments from the first $500 million allocated are scheduled to go out the first week in October to people over the age of 70, or their designated survivors if the internees were alive when the legislation was passed in 1988. A second $500 million will be paid beginning October 1991, with the remaining payments to be sent the following year.

Returning Home Was Difficult for Many After Release from the Camps

Page Smith

The order that Japanese Americans be excluded from military areas on the West Coast of the United States was lifted in January 1945. In the following selection, a historian explains that many evacuees, returning to their homes, found that they were unwelcome or that their businesses were no longer viable. The author offers a number of examples of how, following evacuation, farms owned by Japanese Americans were vandalized or neglected. In other instances, returned evacuees found that locals refused to do business with them or, even worse, threatened violence. Officials of the War Relocation Authority, in charge of the camps and then resettlement, tried to smooth over the process of return, as did some interested and concerned neighbors. Page Smith was a

SOURCE. Page Smith, "The Return—Shushoku," *Democracy on Trial: The Japanese American Evacuation and Relocation in World War II*, Simon & Schuster, 1995, pp. 403–408. Reprinted with the permission of Simon & Schuster, Inc. and Brockman, Inc. Copyright © 1995.

professor of history at William and Mary College and the University of California, Santa Cruz. His books include the eight-volume *People's History of the United States* and *Dissenting Opinions*.

In the immediate aftermath of evacuation [in 1942], forays against abandoned Japanese farms were motivated primarily by simple hostility. Often there was random destruction; things smashed and broken for the pleasure of it. On farms that remained abandoned, many of those who had visited ruin on houses and barns, in [historian Edward H.] Spicer's words, "now went with a view to appropriating anything which their own establishments might lack. Evacuee possessions of easily movable nature had long since been wrecked or stolen, but doors could be removed and carried away for use in the marauders' own houses, window frames were utilized, sinks were appropriated, toilets uprooted and carried away, and built-in shelves were taken apart and the boards taken away."

Shig Doi . . . was a member of the 442nd Combat Team [a US Army unit made up of mostly Japanese Americans]. When the Exclusionary Ban was lifted [in January 1945], Shig Doi's family was one of the first to leave Tule Lake. The senior Doi, having owned his land through his son, had leased it for the duration of the war and was eager to reclaim it. The land had passed through several hands before the raising of the ban and its present tenants were reluctant to give it up. A Caucasian friend told them of a plan to burn down the Dois' packing shed. Doi's sons were on the alert with a fire hose and quickly doused the flames. The following night a shotgun was fired at the farmhouse but the Dois stood fast, refusing to be frightened away and the attacks stopped. The fact that three of their sons were in the service (one of them—Shig—in the famous 442nd) doubtlessly played a part in the ending of the harassment.

The Florin [California] area . . . was an area of marginal land, of small, family-sized farms where the Japanese by heroic efforts raised Tokay grapes and strawberries. The farms in the Florin region had suffered severely from vandalism, in large part because no substitute operators could be found who were prepared to undertake the intensive labor required to produce even a modest return. Those farms that had found tenants, however indifferently maintained, were in far better condition than those that had remained unoccupied. When evacuees from the Florin area began to return, they encountered determined resistance. A War Relocation Authority [WRA] official, visiting the district in March 1945, when evacuees were just starting to return, was appalled at the condition of many of the farms and dismayed at evidence that the Caucasian ranchers were trying to frighten off returnees. The official was confronted by the charred ruins of the Fumi Mukai Fujimoro ranch house and barn, consumed in a suspicious night fire during the owners' temporary absence. The Takeoka brothers owned a nearby ranch and had just returned to occupy it. The Fujimoro fire so alarmed them that they had decided to leave the area. As they were driving away they were intercepted by the official, who expostulated with them, urging them to remain, "pointing out that these cowardly acts were a desperate attempt to frighten away the first evacuees to return, and that courage to face these pioneering hazards until more of the evacuee farmers returned would be worth the effort." By staying they would demonstrate that they were determined to reclaim what was rightfully theirs and thereby encourage others. "When half a dozen adjoining farms were occupied by their owners, night terrorists would hesitate to attack. . . . The

> The official was confronted by the charred ruins of the Fumi Mukai Fujimoro ranch house and barn.

Takeokas turned around and resumed control of their property."

The WRA supervisor was right; the nighttime raids stopped. The owners had demonstrated their resilience. In the words of the supervisor: "They said that by rotation of other crops, by experimenting, by working a little harder, they could get along—it was good to be home again, even if they had to start out once again as they had years ago when they had taken over unimproved or hay land and made it productive." Perhaps the determinative phrase here was "home again." Many of the Japanese prior to Pearl Harbor had thought of Japan as home. The experience of being uprooted and carried off to the relocation camps had changed the meaning of the word.

> The experience of being uprooted and carried off to the relocation camps had changed the meaning of the word ['home'].

Local Citizens' Groups Helped Returning Evacuees

It was soon evident that it was important to get a kind of critical mass of evacuees in communities around whom "local committees of fair-minded citizens who were concerned about racial prejudice and anxious to assist the returning evacuees in their problems of community adjustment" could rally. "Unless such a group was physically present in the evacuated area, it would be like battling racial intolerance in a vacuum." So you needed the combination—enough evacuees to constitute a kind of critical mass and the local organization or consortium of organizations ready and willing to help in whatever way they could.

The tactic developed by the War Relocation Authority was similar to that used by the Association of Southern Women to Prevent Lynching [murderous attacks, usually in the form of hangings, on African Americans]:

the establishment of a network to make known any and every anti-Japanese incident and to immediately dispatch someone in authority to investigate the episode and call on local authorities for assistance in making clear that such actions would not be tolerated and, in the event that local law enforcement individuals or agencies were not responsive, an appeal to higher authorities, accompanied by copious publicity.

Many Americans echoed this barber's sentiment that people of Japanese descent not return to their former places of residence and work even after the war had ended. (**Corbis Corporation.**)

One of the most conspicuous obstacles was Dave Beck, head of the International Teamsters Union and associate of mobsters. Beck encouraged a Teamster boycott of Japanese farm products, whereupon the Author-

> When . . . merchants posted signs in the windows of their stores saying 'No Jap Trade Wanted,' the Authority encouraged the local Japanese to take their business to the neighboring community.

ity sent a marketing specialist into the area to assist evacuees in finding other outlets for their produce. When Hood River Valley [Oregon] merchants posted signs in the windows of their stores saying "No Jap Trade Wanted," the Authority encouraged the local Japanese to take their business to the neighboring community of the Dalles, which was glad to have it. The "No Jap Trade Wanted" signs in Hood River Valley soon disappeared. Often an inquiry from an Authority official or an interested Caucasian citizen would be enough to have an unfriendly sign removed. When [WRA director Dillon S.] Myer and the assistant director of the San Francisco office, Robert Cozzens, traveled up the San Joaquin Valley from Los Angeles to Sacramento to see for themselves what kind of reception returning evacuees were receiving, they found only one family, threatened by random rifle shots, which planned to move as a consequence.

Stopping at a fruit stand where the packing boxes from the Poston [Arizona] center were still in evidence, Myer and Cozzens visited with the family. When the mother appeared from the fields, Myer asked her if she was glad to be home. "No!" was the reply. When Myer asked her why she said: "Too much work!"

Returning Home to Destruction

Peter Tsuchiyama had a poultry ranch at Downey, California, which he leased to a "Mr. J." (so identified in the War Relocation Authority's report) [during his internment]. J., unable to make a go of the venture, leased it to "K. and L." With the rent five months in arrears, a new actor appeared, identified only as "N." He was leasing the farm from L. (K. had dropped out) and taking over its operation because of a large feed bill owed him (he represented himself as a feed dealer). In January 1945, when Tsuchiyama returned to his poultry ranch, there were neither chickens nor eggs and "a considerable quantity of equipment missing."

Vashon Island off the Washington coast was a center of Japanese settlement. When the Miyosha family was shipped off to Minidoka Relocation Center in Idaho, they owned a "well-insured" home on the island in which they stored clothing, furniture, and agricultural equipment owned by them and the equipment of four other island evacuee families. With the premises empty, the insurance company canceled the Miyoshas' policy. Two of the Miyosha sons, Masaru and Glenn, who as citizen children held title to the property, had volunteered for the 100th Infantry Battalion and were sent to Italy where Masaru was seriously wounded. On February 1, 1945, when the family was preparing to return to Vashon, their house was burned down by three boys "just for the thrill" as they testified. The two minor boys and their parents agreed to make restitution to the Miyoshas of $1,000 each.

Another victim with the fictitious name of Hideo Mori was living in the San Joaquin Valley [in central California] when the war with Japan began. By his own account, he was an alien and owned a ranch in Yolo and Solano Counties that he had purchased prior to the Alien Land Law of 1913. Sent to the Gila River Relocation Center and going out early in 1944, Mori, "forewarned of the public sentiment" in Yolo and Solano Counties, found a temporary haven with friends in the San Joaquin Valley. From there he appealed to the War Relocation Authority for assistance. During his time in the Gila River camp, he had rented his land to "local Spaniards." In Mori's words, "They milked it for all it was worth, never bothering to keep it up or improve it, knowing that during the term of their lease no one would come to inspect their work." The consequence

> 'Is it not only fair that restitution for such losses incurred as a result of this evacuation . . . be treated by a measure as forceful as our evacuation?'

was that the value of the ranch decreased dramatically. When Mori reclaimed his land he found that the farm equipment that he had accumulated over some thirty years of farming was broken or stolen. Even water faucets had been carried off as well as household belongings and personal property stored in a locked closet of the farmhouse. Doors and windows had been broken and several doors removed from their hinges. "We were evacuated as a wartime measure," Mori wrote, "and as a result of this evacuation we suffered losses from negligence that borders on sabotage and looting such as can be associated with ransacking hordes of an invading army. Is it not only fair that restitution for such losses incurred as a result of this evacuation—proper restitution to put us back on the economic status from which we were forced—be treated by a measure as forceful as our evacuation?"

The letter was addressed to the director of the War Relocation Authority and the director replied to Mori that while "deeply disturbed to learn of this damage," the War Relocation Authority simply did not have funds to make up such losses. That could only be done by Congress.

Nobu Miyamoto had been a prosperous greenhouse and nursery operator in Seattle. He dealt in cut flowers and potted and bedding plants, owned a large, comfortable house, and had numerous smaller buildings and greenhouses. Ordered to evacuate, Miyamoto and his family collected their belongings, locked them in a sturdy building, and left the key and the authority with an old friend and family lawyer. The friend's health was so poor that he was unable to exercise any real supervision of the lessees and when the Miyamoto family returned in the spring of 1945 they found the place looted and the greenhouses with many smashed panes of glass. Miyamoto's inventory of missing possessions included carpenter and plumber tools, flower shop materials, a trunk containing Japanese silks to the value of $1,500, and a ring valued at the same price.

> An especially offensive act to Japanese from the area was the vandalizing of the Nichiren Buddhist Church in Los Angeles.

Vandalized Farms, Homes, and Religious Centers

An especially offensive act to Japanese from the area was the vandalizing of the Nichiren Buddhist Church in Los Angeles, which was used as a storehouse for the belongings of its evacuated members. When a War Relocation Authority officer visited the church with a member, Mrs. Itano, they encountered in Mrs. Itano's words "a hopeless mass of deliberate destruction. . . . Nothing was untouched. Sewing machines were ruined, furniture broken, mirrors smashed to smithereens . . . household goods scattered helter-skelter, trunks broken open, albums, pictures . . . thrown to the four winds." In addition to the wanton destruction, everything of any possible value had been carried off—electric irons, sewing machines, refrigerators, washing machines, radios, Persian rugs, typewriters.

When Wilson Makabe, wounded in Italy [during the war], arrived in Florida, via a hospital ship in December 1944, he was given a free phone call. He called his brother George, still working in Idaho, and George told him that the family home in Loomis had been burned down just hours after the words had gone out on the radio that the Japanese in the relocation centers could return to the West Coast. "When he told me that," Makabe recalled, ". . . oh, you can't describe the feeling. I remember the pain and the hurt, the suffering in the hospitals in Italy— that was nothing compared to this. I cried for the first time. All that time in the hospital I don't remember shedding a tear, but I cried that night. . . . It was a big house where all of us grew up, and I remember a big dining room that fed all the help at one time, so that we would have as many as twenty or more people sitting around."

One episode from his return to Loomis stuck in Makabe's memory. When he stopped at the Loomis filling station for gas, the owner came out to help him and after the tank was filled he said to Makabe, "I'd like to talk to you." "Hop in." The two men traveled down the road a way and the station owner said, "Y'know, I was one bastard. I had signs on my service station saying 'No Jap trade wanted.' Now when I see you come back like that [referring to Makabe's amputated leg] I feel so small.' And he was crying."

There were, to be sure, many acts of kindness that helped to offset the random vandalism and threats of violence. Herman Neufeld, a Mennonite farmer, had purchased the land of the Takeuchi family at the time of the evacuation. When they returned, Neufeld tried to purchase nearby land in their name. When neighbors protested, Neufeld moved the family onto his farm, remodeled a chicken house for them, and let them stay for two years until they could "get their feet on the ground."

In Turlock [California], the *hakujin* [white] Winton family opened their home to returnees and had, at one time, five families living on their ranch.

Isamu Nakamura recalled that on his way home from the relocation center in Colorado he was forced to spend the night in Turlock. When he could find no hotel that would provide a room, the friendly local sheriff, a retired Methodist minister, offered to put him up for the night in the women's cell at the jail.

Some convalescing *hakujin* veterans were enlisted by [California activist] Josephine Duveneck to go to stores that displayed "No Japs Served Here" signs and suggest that they be taken down. When volunteers received word of particular families that were due to return to an area, they traveled to the town or section of a city where the returnees were headed to enlist leaders of the community in preventing any untoward incidents and, hopefully, to ensure welcomes.

The Supreme Court Decides That the Relocation and Internment of Japanese Americans Is Constitutional

Harlan F. Stone

The decision to remove Japanese Americans from the West Coast was challenged in court several times by people who believed that the order violated their rights as American citizens. One such challenge came from Gordon Hirabayashi, a student at the University of Washington in Seattle. In 1942, Hirabayashi refused to accept the curfew order that was a prelude to relocation, thinking that to do so would amount to a voluntary abandonment of his rights as a US citizen. Rather than simply defy the order, Hirabayashi

---

SOURCE. Harlan F. Stone, "*Hirabayashi v. United States,* 320 U.S. 81," Justia.com, 1943. Supreme.justia.com.

turned himself in and was eventually convicted in a local court of curfew violations. His appeal ultimately reached the US Supreme Court. The court's decision, rendered in 1943, makes up the following selection. The Supreme Court determined that the United States had the right to uphold curfew violations and relocation orders directed at a specific ethnic group in a time of war. It also claimed that, in a period when both Congress and the president had adopted measures to respond to imminent war threats, the principle of equality for all ethnic groups was of secondary importance. Gordon Hirabayashi went on to serve a sentence at a work camp in Arizona until 1945. Harlan F. Stone was chief justice of the US Supreme Court.

Appellant, an American citizen of Japanese ancestry, was convicted in the district court of violating the Act of Congress of March 21, 1942, which makes it a misdemeanor knowingly to disregard restrictions made applicable by a military commander to persons in a military area prescribed by him as such, all as authorized by an Executive Order of the President.

The questions for our decision are whether the particular restriction violated, namely, that all persons of Japanese ancestry residing in such an area be within their place of residence daily between the hours of 8:00 p.m. and 6:00 a.m., was adopted by the military commander in the exercise of an unconstitutional delegation by Congress of its legislative power, and whether the restriction unconstitutionally discriminated between citizens of Japanese ancestry and those of other ancestries in violation of the Fifth Amendment.

> [Appelant contends that] the Fifth Amendment prohibits the discrimination made between citizens of Japanese descent and those of other ancestry. . .

The indictment is in two counts. The second charges that appellant, being a person of Japanese ancestry, had on a specified date, contrary to a restriction promulgated

Gordon Hirabayashi (right) sought the protection of the Fifth Amendment in his refusal to obey curfew laws for Japanese Americans in 1942. (**Corbis Corporation.**)

by the military commander of the Western Defense Command, Fourth Army, failed to remain in his place of residence in the designated military area between the hours of 8:00 o'clock P.M. and 6:00 A.M. The first count charges that appellant, on May 11 and 12, 1942, had, contrary to a Civilian Exclusion Order issued by the military commander, failed to report to the Civil Control Station within the designated area, it appearing that appellant's required presence there was a preliminary step to the exclusion from that area of persons of Japanese ancestry.

Hirabayashi's Claims

[The] appellant asserted that the indictment should be dismissed because he was an American citizen who had never been a subject of and had never borne allegiance to the Empire of Japan, and also because the Act of March 21, 1942, was an unconstitutional delegation of Congressional power. On the trial to a jury, it appeared that appellant was born in Seattle in 1918, of Japanese parents who had come from Japan to the United States, and who had never afterward returned to Japan; that he was educated in the Washington public schools, and, at the time of his arrest was a senior in the University of Washington; that he had never been in Japan or had any association with Japanese residing there.

The evidence showed that appellant had failed to report to the Civil Control Station on May 11 or May 12, 1942, as directed, to register for evacuation from the military area. He admitted failure to do so, and stated it had at all times been his belief that he would be waiving his rights as an American citizen by so doing. The evidence also showed that, for like reason, he was away from his place of residence after 8:00 P.M. on May 9, 1942. The jury returned a verdict of guilty on both counts, and appellant was sentenced to imprisonment for a term of three months on each, the sentences to run concurrently. . . .

Appellant does not deny that he knowingly failed to obey the curfew order as charged in the second count of the indictment, or that the order was authorized by the terms of Executive Order No. 9066, or that the challenged Act of Congress purports to punish with criminal penalties disobedience of such an order. His contentions are only that Congress unconstitutionally delegated its legislative power to the military commander by authorizing him to impose the challenged regulation, and that, even if the regulation were in other respects lawfully authorized, the Fifth Amendment prohibits the discrimination made between citizens of Japanese descent and those of other ancestry. . . .

The Government Was Right to Act

Although the results of the attack on Pearl Harbor were not fully disclosed until much later, it was known that the damage was extensive, and that the Japanese, by their successes, had gained a naval superiority over our forces in the Pacific which might enable them to seize Pearl Harbor, our largest naval base and the last stronghold of defense lying between Japan and the west coast. That reasonably prudent men charged with the responsibility of our national defense had ample ground for concluding that they must face the danger of invasion, take measures against it, and, in making the choice of measures, consider our internal situation, cannot be doubted.

> In the critical days of March, 1942, the danger to our war production by sabotage and espionage in this area seems obvious.

The challenged orders were defense measures for the avowed purpose of safeguarding the military area in question, at a time of threatened air raids and invasion by the Japanese forces, from the danger of sabotage and espionage. As the curfew was made applicable to citizens residing in the area only if they were of Japanese ancestry, our inquiry must be whether, in the light of all the facts and circumstances, there was any substantial basis for the conclusion, in which Congress and the military commander united, that the curfew as applied was a protective measure necessary to meet the threat of sabotage and espionage which would substantially affect the war effort and which might reasonably be expected to aid a threatened enemy invasion. The alternative, which appellant insists must be accepted, is for the military authorities to impose the curfew on all citizens within the military area, or on none. In a case of threatened danger requiring prompt action, it is a choice between inflicting obviously needless hardship on the many or sitting passive and unresisting in the presence of the threat. We think that constitutional government, in time of war, is not so powerless and does not compel so hard a choice if those charged with the responsibility of our national defense have reasonable ground for believing that the threat is real.

When the orders were promulgated, there was a vast concentration, within Military Areas No. 1 and 2, of installations and facilities for the production of military equipment, especially ships and airplanes. Important Army and Navy bases were located in California and Washington. Approximately one-fourth of the total value of the major aircraft contracts then let by Government procurement officers were to be performed in the State of California. California ranked second, and Washington fifth, of all the states of the Union with respect to the value of shipbuilding contracts to be performed.

In the critical days of March, 1942, the danger to our war production by sabotage and espionage in this area seems obvious. The German invasion of the Western European countries had given ample warning to the world of the menace of the "fifth column" [spies]. Espionage by persons in sympathy with the Japanese Government had been found to have been particularly effective in the surprise attack on Pearl Harbor. At a time of threatened Japanese attack upon this country, the nature of our inhabitants' attachments to the Japanese enemy was consequently a matter of grave concern. Of the 126,000 persons of Japanese descent in the United States, citizens and non-citizens, approximately 112,000 resided in California, Oregon and Washington at the time of the adoption of the military regulations. Of

> "Like every military control of the population of a dangerous zone in war time, it necessarily involves some infringement of individual liberty."

these, approximately two-thirds are citizens because born in the United States. Not only did the great majority of such persons reside within the Pacific Coast states, but they were concentrated in or near three of the large cities, Seattle, Portland and Los Angeles, all in Military Area No. 1.

There is support for the view that social, economic and political conditions which have prevailed since the close of the last century, when the Japanese began to come to this country in substantial numbers, have intensified their solidarity and have in large measure prevented their assimilation as an integral part of the white population. In addition, large numbers of children of Japanese parentage are sent to Japanese language schools outside the regular hours of public schools in the locality. Some of these schools are generally believed to be sources of Japanese nationalistic propaganda, cultivating allegiance to Japan. Considerable numbers, estimated to be approximately 10,000, of American-born children of Japanese parentage have been sent to Japan for all or a part of their education.

Reasons to Be Concerned About Japanese Americans

Congress and the Executive, including the military commander, could have attributed special significance, in its bearing on the loyalties of persons of Japanese descent, to the maintenance by Japan of its system of dual citizenship. Children born in the United States of Japanese alien parents, and especially those children born before December 1, 1924, are, under many circumstances, deemed, by Japanese law, to be citizens of Japan. No official census of those whom Japan regards as having thus retained Japanese citizenship is available, but there is ground for the belief that the number is large.

The large number of resident alien Japanese, approximately one-third of all Japanese inhabitants of the country, are of mature years and occupy positions of influence in Japanese communities. The association of influential Japanese residents with Japanese Consulates has been deemed a ready means for the dissemination of propaganda and for the maintenance of the influence of the Japanese Government with the Japanese population in this country.

As a result of all these conditions affecting the life of the Japanese, both aliens and citizens, in the Pacific Coast area, there has been relatively little social intercourse between them and the white population. The restrictions, both practical and legal, affecting the privileges and opportunities afforded to persons of Japanese extraction residing in the United States have been sources of irritation, and may well have tended to increase their isolation, and in many instances their attachments to Japan and its institutions.

Viewing these data in all their aspects, Congress and the Executive could reasonably have concluded that these conditions have encouraged the continued attachment of members of this group to Japan and Japanese institutions.

The Need for Curfews

These are only some of the many considerations which those charged with the responsibility for the national defense could take into account in determining the nature and extent of the danger of espionage and sabotage in the event of invasion or air raid attack. The extent of that danger could be definitely known only after the event, and after it was too late to meet it. Whatever views we may entertain regarding the loyalty to this country of the citizens of Japanese ancestry, we cannot reject as unfounded the judgment of the military authorities and of Congress that there were disloyal members of that population, whose number and strength could not be precisely and quickly ascertained. We cannot say that the war-making branches of the Government did not have ground for believing that in a critical hour such persons could not readily be isolated and separately dealt with, and constituted a menace to the national defense and safety, which demanded that prompt and adequate measures be taken to guard against it.

Appellant does not deny that, given the danger, a curfew was an appropriate measure against sabotage. It is an obvious protection against the perpetration of sabotage most readily committed during the hours of darkness. If it was an appropriate exercise of the war power, its validity is not impaired because it has restricted the citizen's liberty. Like every military control of the population of a dangerous zone in war time, it necessarily involves some infringement of individual liberty, just as does the police establishment of fire lines during a fire, or the confinement of people to their houses during an air raid alarm—neither of which could be thought to be an infringement of constitutional right. Like them, the validity of the restraints of the curfew order depends on all the conditions which obtain at the time the curfew is imposed and which support the order imposing it.

But appellant insists that the exercise of the power is inappropriate and unconstitutional because it discriminates against citizens of Japanese ancestry, in violation of the Fifth Amendment. The Fifth Amendment contains no equal protection clause, and it restrains only such discriminatory legislation by Congress as amounts to a denial of due process. Congress may hit at a particular danger where it is seen, without providing for others which are not so evident or so urgent.

This Time, Ethnic Discrimination Is Justified

Distinctions between citizens solely because of their ancestry are, by their very nature, odious to a free people whose institutions are founded upon the doctrine of equality. For that reason, legislative classification or discrimination based on race alone has often been held to be a denial of equal protection. We may assume that these considerations would be controlling here were it not for the fact that the danger of espionage and sabotage, in time of war and of threatened invasion, calls upon the military authorities to scrutinize every relevant fact bearing on the loyalty of populations in the danger areas. Because racial discriminations are in most circumstances irrelevant, and therefore prohibited, it by no means follows that, in dealing with the perils of war, Congress and the Executive are wholly precluded from taking into account those facts and circumstances which are relevant to measures for our national defense and for the successful prosecution of the war, and which may, in fact, place citizens of one ancestry in a different category from others. "We must never forget that it is *a constitution* we are expounding," "a constitution intended to endure for ages to come, and, consequently, to be adapted to the various *crises* of human affairs." [*17 U.S. 407, 17 U.S. 415*]. [As an earlier Supreme Court decision noted:]

> The aim of Congress and the Executive was the protection against sabotage . . . in areas thought to be in danger of Japanese invasion and air attack.

The adoption by Government, in the crisis of war and of threatened invasion, of measures for the public safety, based upon the recognition of facts and circumstances which indicate that a group of one national extraction may menace that safety more than others, is not wholly beyond the limits of the Constitution, and is not to be condemned merely because, in other and in most circumstances, racial distinctions are irrelevant.

Here, the aim of Congress and the Executive was the protection against sabotage of war materials and utilities in areas thought to be in danger of Japanese invasion and air attack. We have stated in detail facts and circumstances with respect to the American citizens of Japanese ancestry residing on the Pacific Coast which support the judgment of the war-waging branches of the Government that some restrictive measure was urgent. We cannot say that these facts and circumstances, considered in the particular war setting, could afford no ground for differentiating citizens of Japanese ancestry from other groups in the United States. The fact alone that attack on our shores was threatened by Japan, rather than another enemy power, set these citizens apart from others who have no particular associations with Japan.

The Supreme Court's Decisions Supporting Internment Were Rightfully Overturned

Kermit L. Hall and John J. Patrick

In the following selection, legal scholars examine the 1943 case in which the Supreme Court ruled the relocation of Japanese Americans to be constitutional. The authors point out, however, that not all nine Supreme Court justices were comfortable with the ruling. They further explain that two Supreme Court decisions against Japanese Americans were overturned in 1983. A reexamination of the cases determined that the Supreme Court had made mistaken decisions in both. Kermit L. Hall's distinguished career in academia included six well-regarded works on legal history as well as the presidency of the State University of New York, Albany.

SOURCE. Kermit L. Hall and John J. Patrick, "Internment of Japanese Americans During World War II," *The Pursuit of Justice: Supreme Court Decisions That Shaped America*, Oxford University Press, 2006, pp. 95–96, 98. © 2006 The Annenberg Foundation Trust at Sunnylands. By permission of Oxford University Press, Inc.

John J. Patrick is a professor of education at Indiana University. His books include *An Oxford Guide to the U.S. Government*.

The internment of the Japanese Americans [during World War II] certainly raised serious issues about constitutional rights. For example, the Constitution's Fifth Amendment says, "No person shall be . . . deprived of life, liberty, or property, without due process of law." Had the federal government deprived the interned Japanese Americans of their Fifth Amendment rights? Or did the wartime emergency justify the federal government's placement of extraordinary limitations on the constitutional rights of a particular group of Americans? Federal courts soon confronted these critical issues about the government's use of war powers and the constitutional rights of Japanese Americans.

> 'I must maintain the democratic standards for which this nation lives.'

The first Japanese American internment case to come before the U.S. Supreme Court concerned Gordon Hirabayashi, a U.S. citizen born and raised in Seattle, Washington. Prior to his problems with the federal government, he was a highly regarded student at the University of Washington in Seattle.

Hirabayashi had been arrested and convicted for violating General [John L.] DeWitt's curfew order and for refusing to register at a control station in preparation for transportation to an internment camp. His noncompliance with federal regulations was based strongly on principle. Hirabayashi believed that the President's executive orders, and the federal laws enacted in support of them, were racially discriminatory violations of the U.S. Constitution. He later said: "I must maintain the democratic standards for which this nation lives. . . . I am objecting to the principle of this order which denies the rights of human beings, including citizens."

The Supreme Court Decision

The Court unanimously upheld the curfew law for Japanese Americans living in Military Area 1 and ruled that the federal government had appropriately used its war powers under the Constitution. It did not directly confront the issue of whether the exclusion and internment order violated Hirabayashi's Fifth Amendment rights, as the Court focused on the constitutional justifications for the curfew law during a wartime crisis, a law that Hirabayashi clearly had violated.

Writing for the Court, Chief Justice Harlan Fiske Stone recognized that discrimination based upon race was "odious to a free people whose institutions are founded upon the doctrine of equality." In this case, however, Stone ruled that the need to protect national security in time of war compelled consideration of race and ancestry as reasons for confinement of a certain group of people. The chief justice wrote, "We cannot close our eyes to the fact. . . . that in time of war residents having ethnic affiliations with an invading enemy may be a greater source of danger than those of a different ancestry."

Although the Court's decision in Hirabayashi was unanimous, Justice Frank Murphy did not wholeheartedly endorse it, and he wrote a concurring opinion that verged on dissent. In fact, Murphy had at first decided to write a dissenting opinion, but Chief Justice Stone, with help from Justice Felix Frankfurter, talked him out of it. Frankfurter argued that in a socially sensitive case like this one, it was important for the Court to present an appearance of unity. Nonetheless, Murphy's concurrence was sprinkled with sharply stated reservations about the Court's opinion. For example, Murphy expressed great concern that "we have sustained a substantial restriction of the personal liberty of citizens of the United States based on the accident of race or ancestry. . . . In my opinion, this goes to the very brink of constitutional power." . . .

The Tide Turns

Shortly after the end of World War II, Japanese Americans who had been relocated to internment camps filed grievances with the federal government to seek compensation for unjust treatment. In 1948, Congress responded by enacting the Japanese American Evacuation Claims Act, which provided compensation to internees who had evidence to prove the amount of their property losses. However, no more than $37 million was paid in compensation, despite estimates that Japanese Americans had suffered property losses totaling more than $400 million. Furthermore, compensation was not provided for losses of income or profits that they would have earned during the period of detention in the relocation centers.

> The commission found no evidence of espionage or sabotage by any of the Japanese Americans.

In 1980, Congress established the Commission on Wartime Relocation and Internment of Civilians to investigate the treatment of Japanese Americans during World War II and to make recommendations about financial compensation to the victims. After careful examination of the evidence, including testimony from 750 witnesses, the commission issued a report on February 25, 1983. The commission found no evidence of espionage or sabotage by any of the Japanese Americans. In addition, it noted that officials of both the Federal Bureau of Investigation and the Office of Naval Intelligence had opposed the exclusion and internment orders because they believed the Japanese Americans collectively posed no threat to the country's security. The report con-

Photo on following page: In the case of *Hirabayashi v. United States*, Justice Frank Murphy did not wholeheartedly endorse the unanimous decision of the court, writing a concurring opinion that bordered on dissent. (Time & Life Pictures/Getty Images.)

cluded: "A grave injustice was done to American citizens and resident aliens of Japanese ancestry who, without individual review or any probative evidence against them, were excluded, removed, and detained by the United States during World War II."

In January 1983, Gordon Hirabayashi and Fred Korematsu [whose conviction for refusing detention was also, in 1944, upheld by the Supreme Court] petitioned the federal judiciary to vacate and overturn their criminal convictions. They claimed procedural errors and faulty use of information had influenced the judicial decisions against them. First Korematsu and later Hirabayashi achieved reversal of their convictions, which were erased from federal court records.

In 1988, on the basis of the 1983 report by the federal government commission, Congress officially recognized the wrongs done to Americans of Japanese ancestry by the exclusion and relocation policies. It enacted legislation to provide twenty thousand dollars in compensation to each person still living who had been detained in a relocation center or to the heirs of deceased victims. More than forty-six years after the fateful executive orders that had victimized them were issued, the Japanese American community received a belated token of compensatory justice.

Many Japanese Americans Demonstrated Their Loyalty Through Military Service

Ronald Takaki

The following selection explains that many thousands of Japanese Americans joined their fellow citizens in active military service during World War II. Many of them, and the first to join up, were Nisei, or second-generation Japanese Americans, from Hawaii. There, Japanese Americans were not subject to internment because they made up a large proportion of the population of the islands and were necessary to its economy. Many of these troops used their Japanese language skills as translators. For Nisei sent to the internment camps on the US mainland, the question of military service was more difficult. In 1943, all internees were

SOURCE. Ronald Takaki, "Diversity: The Watershed of World War II," *Strangers from a Distant Shore: A History of Asian Americans*, Back Bay Books, 1989, pp. 399–403. Reproduced by permission of Little, Brown and Company and the Ward & Balkin Agency, Inc.

forced to answer a questionnaire concerning their loyalty. Many of the young men who claimed on the questionnaire that they were willing to serve in combat duty and had "unqualified allegiance" to the United States found that they were then subject to the military draft. Others joined up voluntarily. As the author notes, Nisei troops from both Hawaii and the mainland often performed heroically in Europe, though their contributions were not always recognized upon their return. Ronald Takaki was a professor of Asian American studies at the University of California, Berkeley. His books include *A Different Mirror: A History of Multicultural America* and *Double Victory: A Multicultural History of America in World War II*.

D uring the war, 33,000 Nisei [second generation, US-born Japanese Americans] served in the U.S. Armed Forces. They believed participation in the defense of their country was the best way to express their loyalty and to fulfill their obligation as citizens. Several thousand of them were members of the Military Intelligence Service [MIS], functioning as interpreters and translators on the Pacific front. Armed with Japanese language skills, they provided an invaluable service, translating captured Japanese documents, including battle plans, lists of Imperial Navy ships, and Japanese secret codes. Richard Sakakida's translation of Japanese plans for a landing on Bataan [in the Philippines] made it possible for American tanks to ambush the invaders as they landed. Nisei soldiers volunteered for service with Merrill's Marauders in Burma; one of their officers described their heroic work: "During battles they crawled up close enough to be able to hear Jap officers' commands and to make verbal translations to our soldiers. They tapped lines, listened in on radios, translated documents and papers, made spot translations of messages and field orders. . . ." As members of the MIS, Nisei soldiers participated in the invasion of Okinawa. Two of them, Hiroshi Kobashigawa and Frank Higashi were worried about their

Photo on following page: Japanese Americans often helped to administer the internment camps and received recognition from camp officials not only for their aid but for their loyalty as Americans (Amber Tiffany/Furuya family, San Diego, CA.)

WAR RELOCATION AUTHORITY
Colorado River Relocation Center
Poston, Arizona

In reply, please refer to:

December 30, 1943

TO WHOM IT MAY CONCERN:

It gives me great pleasure to highly recommend Mr. Roy Furuya.

Mr. Furuya while a resident of this project has unselfishly given of his time and effort to help make this project a success. Since his arrival he has held increasingly more responsible administrative positions. Until at the present time he holds one of the top administrative positions in the management of this unit for almost 9,000 people. He has the full confidence of the administration and has proven without doubt his ability to accept responsibility and to get the job done.

His loyalty as an American citizen is above question which fact he has proven on numerous occasions. He was the main "spark plug" in the program of recruiting volunteers for the American army and was directly responsible for the volunteering of many of the young men.

I recommend Mr. Furuya without reservation and feel that he will be a distinct asset to any community or organization with which he may become attached.

Ralph M. Gelvin
Associate Project Director

families in Okinawa. Both of them had been born in the United States and had parents who had returned to Okinawa before the outbreak of the war. When American soldiers landed in Okinawa, they found the people hiding in caves: Okinawans had been told by the Japanese military it would be better for them to be dead than to be captured, and the Okinawans were afraid they would be tortured, raped, and killed by the Americans. In his family's home village, Kobashigawa was relieved to find his mother, sister, and three younger brothers safe in a civilian refugee camp. Higashi found his father in the hills of northern Okinawa during a mop-up operation and carried him on his back to the village. Nisei soldiers like Kobashigawa and Higashi rescued their own families and also persuaded many Japanese soldiers to surrender. General Charles Willoughby, chief of intelligence in the Pacific, estimated that Nisei MIS contributions shortened the war by two years.

Fighting on Two Fronts

Nisei soldiers also helped to win the war in Europe. In 1942, while General [John L.] DeWitt evacuated the Japanese on the West Coast, General [Delos C.] Emmons recommended the formation of a battalion of Hawaiian Nisei—the 100th Battalion. After training at Camp McCoy in Wisconsin and Camp Shelby in Mississippi, fourteen hundred Nisei of the 100th Battalion were sent to northern Africa and then to Italy in September 1943. They participated in the Italian campaign until the following March. Three hundred of them were killed and 650 wounded. The 100th was called the "Purple Heart Battalion." In June [1944], the 100th Battalion merged with the newly arrived 442nd Regimental Combat Team, composed of Nisei from Hawaii and from internment camps on the mainland. The Nisei soldiers experienced bloody fighting at Luciana, Livorno, and the Arno River [in Italy], where casualties totaled 1,272 men—more than one fourth of the regiment. After the battle at the Arno River, they were sent to France, where they took the town of Bruyeres from the German troops in heavy house-to-house fighting. Then they were ordered to rescue the Texan "Lost Battalion," 211 men surrounded by German troops in the Vosges Mountains. "If we advanced a hundred yards, that was a good day's job," recalled a Nisei soldier describing the rescue mission. "We'd dig in again, move up another hundred yards, and dig in. That's how we went. It took us a whole week to get to the Lost Battalion. It was just a tree-to-tree fight." At the end of the week of fighting, the 442nd had suffered eight hundred casualties. When the trapped Texans finally saw the

> 'We were never so glad to see anyone as those fighting Japanese Americans.'

Nisei soldiers, some broke into sobs. One of the rescued soldiers remembered the moment: "[The Germans] would hit us from one flank and then the other, then from the front and the rear . . . we were never so glad to see anyone as those fighting Japanese Americans."

The "Go for Broke" Boys

Nisei soldiers went on to take the Gothic Line in northern Italy and then in April 1945 assaulted German troops on Mount Nebbione. "Come on, you guys, go for broke!" they shouted as they charged directly into the fire of enemy machine guns. Captain Daniel Inouye crawled to the flank of an emplacement and pulled the pin on his grenade. "As I drew my arm back, all in a flash of light and dark I saw him, that faceless German," he remembered.

And even as I cocked my arm to throw, he fired and his rifle grenade smashed into my right elbow and exploded and all but tore my arm off. I looked at it, stunned and unbelieving. It dangled there by a few bloody shreds of

The Nisei soldiers of the 442nd regiment earned 18,143 individual decorations during World War II, risking their lives in order to prove their loyalty to the United States. (Time & Life Pictures/Getty Images.)

tissue, my grenade still clenched in a fist that suddenly didn't belong to me any more. . . . I swung around to pry the grenade out of that dead fist with my left hand. Then I had it free and I turned to throw and the German was reloading his rifle. But this time I beat him. My grenade blew up in his face and I stumbled to my feet, closing on the bunker, firing my tommy gun left-handed, the useless right arm slapping red and wet against my side.

The war, for the wounded Captain Inouye, was over. Two weeks later, in May 1945, the war in Europe came to an end for everyone. Nisei soldiers of the 442nd had suffered 9,486 casualties, including six hundred killed. "Just think of all those people—of the 990 that went over [with me], not more than 200 of them came back without getting hit," said 442nd veteran Shig Doi. "If you look at the 442nd boys, don't look at their faces, look at their bodies. They got hit hard, some lost their limbs." The 442nd, military observers agreed, was "probably the most decorated unit in United States military history." They had earned 18,143 individual decorations— including one Congressional Medal of Honor, forty-seven Distinguished Service Crosses, 350 Silver Stars, 810 Bronze Stars, and more than thirty-six hundred Purple Hearts. They had given their lives and limbs to prove their loyalty.

> 'You're damn right those Nisei boys have a place in the American heart, now and forever.'

One of the Nisei soldiers explained the meaning of their involvement and their sacrifice in the war. In a letter to a young Japanese woman in Hawaii, he wrote from the European battlefront during the war:

My friends and my family—they mean everything to me. They are the most important reason why I am giving up my education and my happiness to go to fight a war that we never asked for. But our Country is involved in it. Not only that. By virtue of the Japanese attack on our nation, we as American citizens of Japanese ancestry have been mercilessly flogged with criticism and accusations. But I'm not going to take it sitting down! I may not be able to come back. But that matters little. My family and friends—they are the ones who will be able to back their arguments with facts. They are the ones who will be proud. In fact, it is better that we are sent to the front and that a few of us do not return, for the testimony will be stronger in favor of the folks back home.

"They bought an awful hunk of America with their blood," declared General Joseph Stilwell. "You're damn right those Nisei boys have a place in the American heart,

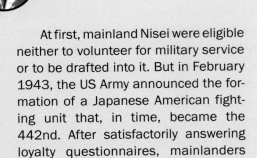

Japanese American Soldiers in World War II

Thousands of Japanese Americans fought for the United States during World War II. The units with which they are commonly associated, the 100th Infantry Battalion and the 442nd Regimental Combat Team, were among the most highly decorated army units of the war. The approximately fourteen thousand men who served in these units received a total of 18,143 medals and were awarded a collective Congressional Medal of Honor, the highest award available to combat troops.

The first Japanese Americans to serve in the World War II era were Nisei from Hawaii. The large numbers of Japanese Americans in Hawaii made large-scale internment impossible, and many of them joined volunteer service units to prove their loyalty. Eventually, some young men were permitted to join the unit that came to be known as the 100th Infantry Battalion. The unit was sent to the mainland for training, destined to take part in the war in Europe. Only a small group of Japanese interpreters and translators took part in the Pacific war against Japan.

At first, mainland Nisei were eligible neither to volunteer for military service or to be drafted into it. But in February 1943, the US Army announced the formation of a Japanese American fighting unit that, in time, became the 442nd. After satisfactorily answering loyalty questionnaires, mainlanders were free to join up. The first induction into the 442nd included three thousand Nisei from Hawaii and eight hundred from the mainland.

The 100th Infantry Battalion was integrated into the 442nd Regimental Combat Team in June 1944. Over the next months, Japanese American troops fought in Italy, France, and eventually Germany. Among their many accomplishments was the rescue of a unit from Texas that was trapped by German forces in late 1944. The 442nd saved the so-called "Lost Battalion" of Texans at a heavy cost in casualties. Another unit of Japanese American soldiers helped to liberate the Dachau concentration camp in Germany in April 1945. Following the war, Nisei veterans continued to serve with great distinction in politics in both Hawaii and the US mainland. They led the process that resulted in Hawaiian statehood in 1959, and several have served in the US Congress.

now and forever." After the war in 1945, General Stilwell flew to California to award the Distinguished Service Cross to Kazuo Masuda. Sergeant Masuda of the 442nd had single-handedly fired a mortar on Nazi positions and had been killed at Cassino, Italy. On the porch of a frame shack in Orange County, General Stilwell pinned the medal on Masuda's sister, Mary, who had recently returned from the internment camp. Several show-business personalities, including Robert Young and Will Rogers, participated in the ceremony, and a young actor, Ronald Reagan, paid tribute to the fallen Nisei soldier:

> Blood that has soaked into the sands of a beach is all of one color. America stands unique in the world, the only country not founded on race, but on a way—an ideal. Not in spite of, but because of our polyglot background, we have had all the strength in the world. That is the American way.

Recognition from the Famous and Humble

The Nisei soldiers had made an impact back home. A Filipino described how his attitude toward Japanese Americans had been turned around by the valor of the Nisei soldiers:

> When Japan bombed Pearl Harbor, Manila, and all parts of the Philippines, I was entirely against the Japanese too. My feeling was 100% against them. But when those Japanese in the war showed their patriotism in favor of this country, I changed my mind. They should not have been taken [to internment camps]. Like the Italians and the Germans, all those born here are citizens. They should not have been suspected as spies.

After the war, on July 15, 1946, on the lawn of the White House, President Harry Truman welcomed home the Nisei soldiers of the 442nd: "You fought for the free nations of the world . . . you fought not only the enemy, you fought prejudice—and you won."

As they stood on the land of their birth, however, they could not be certain they had defeated prejudice in America. Captain Inouye soon discovered they had not won the war at home. He was on his way back to Hawaii in 1945 when he tried to get a haircut in San Francisco. Entering the barbershop with his empty right sleeve pinned to his army jacket covered with ribbons and medals for his military heroism, Captain Inouye was told: "We don't serve Japs here." Another Nisei soldier from Hawaii reflected on the future of his brothers in arms from the mainland. He and his Hawaiian buddies would be returning to the islands to take up "again the threads of life" where they had been left off. But the mainland Nisei soldiers had "no home to return to except the wire-enclosed relocation centers." "They have nothing to look forward to," he observed sadly, "except an even greater fight than that which they are undergoing here in Italy— to win their battle at home against the race-baiters and professional patriots."

Some Japanese Americans Were Insulted by Demands for Loyalty and Calls to Serve

W. Dale Nelson

In the following selection, a Wyoming reporter writes of an event at which former members of the Fair Play Committee spoke, decades after the end of World War II. The Fair Play Committee was formed among some of the Japanese Americans interned at the Heart Mountain camp in Wyoming. Its members refused to allow themselves to be drafted into the US armed forces during World War II on the grounds that they had been treated unfairly through relocation and detention. One went so far as to refer to the loyalty question as "stupid," while others suggested that their experiences might offer lessons for more recent times.

SOURCE. W. Dale Nelson, "Heart Mountain Draft Resisters Speak at UW," *Casper Star Tribune,* April 27, 2003. Trib.com. Copyright © 2003 by W. Dale Nelson. Reprinted by permission of the author.

Heart Mountain draft resisters and their supporters recalled Saturday [April 26, 2003] their "unfair, unjust, immoral and legally questionable" treatment during World War II and said Arab-Americans now face the same thing under the Patriot Act passed by Congress.

Frank Emi, chairman of the Fair Play Committee formed by some inmates of the Wyoming relocation center, said he was 26 and had two young children and a grocery store in Los Angeles when Japan attacked Pearl Harbor.

About 110,000 Japanese-Americans on the West Coast were sent to centers in Arizona, Arkansas, Colorado, Idaho, Utah, Wyoming and inland California under an executive order signed by President Franklin D. Roosevelt.

> 'The real threat to our democracy was at my very doorstep.'

Emi said he had to sell his store "at pennies on the dollar" because of the speed with which he and his family were swept up and moved to Heart Mountain. "They had us over a barrel," he said.

They arrived in Wyoming from Southern California in August, he said, and the first snow fell in September. Temperatures plunged at times to 30 degrees below zero. Their plank-and-tarpaper shacks were not given any insulation until December.

The Fair Play Committee was formed after the camp's inmates were reclassified from 4C, for enemy alien, to 1A, the top classification for the draft. Because of his age and his young family, Emi, like most of the committee's founders, was not subject to the draft.

Yosh Kuromiya, however, was. Kuromiya was an 18-year-old student at Pasadena Junior College when the United States entered the war. Like others in the San Gabriel Valley, he and his family were first held at the Pomona Fair Grounds and then taken to Heart Mountain.

Kuromiya, speaking with Emi at a forum sponsored by the University of Wyoming's [UW] Organization of Active Students Interested in Sociology, said that as a patriotic American he was at first inclined to respond to his country's call, but then came to believe that "the real threat to our democracy was at my very doorstep."

Refusing the Draft

He was one of 63 young men at Heart Mountain who refused to report for induction. They and the seven organizers of the committee were tried and convicted, and sentenced to terms ranging from two to four years. After the war, some of the convictions were reversed and President Harry S. Truman pardoned the draft resisters.

After having had 59 years to reflect, said Kuromiya, he now believes, to paraphrase a thought of Albert Einstein, that "unthinking respect for authority is the greatest enemy of a democracy."

Although some Japanese Americans joined the military, other young men at the Heart Mountain internment camp resisted the prevailing calls for military service and outward displays of loyalty. **(Time & Life Pictures/Getty Images.)**

The No No Boys

The Fair Play Committee was one of the few examples of resistance to the internment orders. Another was the rise of a group of so-called "no no boys." These young men—a total of more than 4,500—answered "no" or refused to fully respond to two questions placed on the loyalty questionnaires that Japanese American internees were asked to fill out in 1943. One question asked whether they were "willing to serve in the armed forces of the United States on combat duty." The other asked internees to "swear unqualified allegiance to the United States of America and . . . forswear any form of allegiance or obedience to the Japanese emperor, or any other foreign government." As punishment, many of the "no no boys" were sent to the fairly restrictive internment camp at Tule Lake, California, along with other "troublesome" internees.

Tak Hoshizaki, another draft resister who was invited to speak at the forum, could not attend but sent a statement that was read by the master of ceremonies, Sandy Root-Elledge, a graduate student in sociology who wrote a master's thesis about Heart Mountain.

"The removal and the unconstitutional incarceration of Americans of Japanese ancestry . . . in 1942 has been in my mind reincarnated 60 years later in the form of the USA Patriot Act of 2002," Hoshizaki said. "Both trample on the constitutional rights of the people of the United States under the guise of wartime necessity."

"This time it is the alienation and prosecution of Americans of Arab/Muslim background," he said.

Emi, Kuromiya and Hoshizaki all live in the Los Angeles area.

Donna Barnes, an associate professor of sociology at the UW, described the three as "remarkable men" who performed what was "truly an act of principle and conscience."

"It is remarkable," said Barnes, "to find people in this kind of hostile environment who would step forth."

Michael Brose, an assistant professor of history, said Japanese-Americans at the time often found themselves "very conflicted" in balancing their loyalty to the United States and their Japanese culture.

> The Fair Play Committee 'took on the draft issue' because it was 'unfair, unjust, immoral and legally questionable.'

Nevertheless, he said, "These people were really the quiet Americans who were very acceptive of American values and patriotic ideals."

Emi said that the Fair Play Committee "took on the draft issue" because it was "unfair, unjust, immoral and legally questionable."

He said that when asked to sign a document stating that he forswore any allegiance to Japan, he declined to sign because as a second-generation American he had never had any such allegiance.

"Under the present circumstances, I cannot answer this question," he wrote on the document. To Saturday's audience, he said, "It was a very stupid question."

CHAPTER 3

Personal Narratives

The Uncertain Weeks Following Pearl Harbor

Yoshiko Uchida

Japanese Americans, as most other Americans, were caught completely by surprise when Imperial Japan attacked the US naval base at Pearl Harbor, Hawaii, on December 7, 1941. Few believed that they would be singled out for special attention by a US government now at war. But, as Yoshiko Uchida writes in the following selection, Japanese American families had to adjust quickly to new realities. Uchida, then a twenty-year-old student at the University of California, Berkeley, remembers finding out that her father had already been detained by the FBI the evening of December 7. She, her mother, and her sister Kay remained unsure of his fate for five days. Eventually, they learned that the senior Uchida was to be sent to a detention camp in Montana. The family then had to learn to adjust to the absence of the man who had guided their household as they faced an uncertain future. Yoshiko Uchida is the author of more than 30 fiction and nonfiction books, including

Photo on previous page: A few personal items sit on a table in a home at an internment camp. **(Getty Images.)**

SOURCE. Yoshiko Uchida, "Pearl Harbor," *Desert Exile: The Uprooting of a Japanese American Family*, University of Washington Press, 1982, pp. 46–50. Copyright © 1982 by the Bancroft Library. Reproduced by permission.

Journey to Topaz: A Story of the Japanese American Evacuation, The Forever Christmas Tree, and *Picture Bride.*

It was one of those rare Sundays when we had no guests for dinner. My parents, sister, and I had just come home from church and were having a quiet lunch when we heard a frenzied voice on the radio break in on the program. The Japanese had attacked Pearl Harbor.

"Oh no," Mama cried out. "It can't be true."

"Of course not," Papa reassured her. "And if it is, it's only the work of a fanatic."

We all agreed with him. Of course it could only be an aberrant act of some crazy irresponsible fool. It never for a moment occurred to any of us that this meant war. As a matter of fact, I was more concerned about my approaching finals at the university than I was with this bizarre news and went to the library to study. When I got there, I found clusters of Nisei [second-generation Japanese American] students anxiously discussing the shocking event. But we all agreed it was only a freak incident and turned our attention to our books. I stayed at the library until 5:00 P.M. giving no further thought to the attack on Pearl Harbor.

When I got home, the house was filled with an uneasy quiet. A strange man sat in our living room and my father was gone. The FBI had come to pick him up, as they had dozens of other Japanese men. Executives of Japanese business firms, shipping lines, and banks, men active in local Japanese associations, teachers of Japanese language schools, virtually every leader of the Japanese American community along the West Coast had been seized almost immediately.

Actually the FBI had come to our house twice, once in the absence of my parents and sister who, still not realizing the serious nature of the attack, had gone out to

Photo on following page: In the days after the attack on Pearl Harbor, Hawaii, many Japanese American families were broken up as the fear of spies spread. (**Getty Images.**)

visit friends. Their absence, I suppose, had been cause for suspicion and the FBI or police had broken in to search our house without a warrant. On returning, my father, believing that we had been burglarized, immediately called the police. Two policemen appeared promptly with three FBI men and suggested that my father check to see if his valuables were missing. They were, of course, undisturbed, but their location was thereby revealed. Two of the FBI men requested that my father accompany them "for a short while" to be questioned, and my father went willingly. The other FBI man remained with my mother and sister to intercept all phone calls and to inform anyone who called that they were indisposed.

> 'Let's leave the porch light on and the screen door unlatched,' Mama said hopefully. 'Maybe Papa will be back later tonight.'

A Visit from the FBI

One policeman stationed himself at the front door and the other at the rear. When two of our white friends came to see how we were, they were not permitted to enter or speak to my mother and sister, who, for all practical purposes, were prisoners in our home.

By the time I came home, only one FBI man remained, but I was alarmed at the startling turn of events during my absence. In spite of her own anxiety, Mama in her usual thoughtful way was serving tea to the FBI agent. He tried to be friendly and courteous, reassuring me that my father would return safely in due time. But I couldn't share my mother's gracious attitude toward him. Papa was gone, and his abrupt custody into the hands of the FBI seemed an ominous portent of worse things to come. I had no inclination to have tea with one of its agents, and went abruptly to my room, slamming the door shut.

Eventually, after a call from headquarters, the FBI agent left, and Mama, Kay, and I were alone at last. Mama made supper and we sat down to eat, but no one was hungry. Without Papa things just weren't the same, and none of us dared voice the fear that sat like a heavy black stone inside each of us.

"Let's leave the porch light on and the screen door unlatched," Mama said hopefully. "Maybe Papa will be back later tonight."

But the next morning the light was still burning, and we had no idea of his whereabouts. All that day and for three days that followed, we had no knowledge of what had happened to my father. And somehow during those days, I struggled through my finals.

It wasn't until the morning of the fifth day that one of the men apprehended with my father, but released because he was an American citizen, called to tell us that my father was being detained with about one hundred other Japanese men at the Immigration Detention Quarters in San Francisco. The following day a postcard arrived from Papa telling us where he was and asking us to send him his shaving kit and some clean clothes. "Don't worry, I'm all right," he wrote, but all we knew for certain was that he was alive and still in San Francisco.

> When it was time to say goodbye, none of us could speak for the ache in our hearts.

A Tense Visit

As soon as permission was granted, we went to visit him at the Immigration Detention Quarters, a drab, dreary institutional structure. We went in, anxious and apprehensive, and were told to wait in a small room while my father was summoned from another part of the building. As I stepped to the door and looked down the dingy hallway, I saw Papa coming toward me with a uniformed guard following close behind. His steps were eager, but he looked worn and tired.

"Papa! Are you all right?"

He hugged each of us.

"I'm all right. I'm fine," he reassured us.

But our joy in seeing him was short-lived, for he told us that he was among a group of ninety men who would be transferred soon to an army internment camp in Missoula, Montana.

"Montana!" we exclaimed. "But we won't be able to see you anymore then."

"I know," Papa said, "but you can write me letters and I'll write you too. Write often, and be very careful—all of you. Kay and Yo, you girls take good care of Mama." His concern was more for us than for himself.

When it was time to say goodbye, none of us could speak for the ache in our hearts. My sister and I began to cry. And it was Mama who was the strong one.

The three of us watched Papa go down the dark hallway with the guard and disappear around a corner. He was gone, and we didn't know if we would ever see him again. There were rumors that men such as my father were to be held as hostages in reprisal for atrocities committed by the Japanese soldiers. If the Japanese killed American prisoners, it was possible my father might be among those killed in reprisal.

> As the oldest citizen of our household, my sister now had to assume responsibility for managing our business affairs.

It was the first time in our lives that Papa had been separated from us against his will. We returned home in silent gloom, my sister dabbing at her eyes and blowing her nose as she drove us back to Berkeley. When we got home, we comforted ourselves by immediately packing and shipping a carton of warm clothing to Papa in Montana, glad for the opportunity to do something to help him.

As soon as our friends heard that my father had been interned, they gathered around to give us support and comfort, and for several days running we had over fifteen callers a day.

Upon reaching Montana, my father wrote immediately, his major concern being whether we would have enough money for our daily needs. He and my mother were now classified as "enemy aliens" and his bank account had been blocked immediately. For weeks there was total confusion regarding the amount that could be withdrawn from such blocked accounts for living expenses, and early reports indicated it would be only $100 a month.

"Withdraw as much as you can from my account," Papa wrote to us. "I don't want you girls to dip into your own savings accounts unless absolutely necessary."

New Responsibilities

As the oldest citizen of our household, my sister now had to assume responsibility for managing our business affairs, and it was not an easy task. There were many important papers and documents we needed, but the FBI had confiscated all of my father's keys, including those to his safe deposit box, and their inaccessibility was a problem for us.

We exchanged a flurry of letters as my father tried to send detailed instructions on how to endorse checks on his behalf; how to withdraw money from his accounts; when and how to pay the premiums on his car and life insurance policies; what to do about filing his income tax returns which he could not prepare without his records; and later, when funds were available, how to purchase defense bonds for him. Another time he asked us to send him a check for a fellow internee who needed a loan.

My father had always managed the business affairs of our household, and my mother, sister, and I were totally unprepared to cope with such tasks. Our confusion and bewilderment were overwhelming, and we could sense my father's frustration and anguish at being unable to help us except through censored letters, and later through internee telegrams which were permitted to discourage letter-writing.

Papa's letters were always in English, not only for the benefit of the censor, but for my sister and me. And we could tell from each one that he was carefully reviewing in his mind every aspect of our lives in Berkeley.

"Don't forget to lubricate the car," he would write. "And be sure to prune the roses in January. Brush Laddie [the family dog] every day and give him a pat for me. Don't forget to send a monthly check to Grandma and take my Christmas offering to church."

In every letter he reassured us about his health, sent greetings to his friends, and expressed concern about members of our church.

"Tell those friends at church whose businesses have been closed not to be discouraged," he wrote in one of his first letters. "Tell them things will get better before long."

And he asked often about his garden.

A University Student Adjusts to Internment

Charles Kikuchi

The following selection consists of excerpts of a diary maintained by Charles Kikuchi, who was a twenty-six-year-old graduate student in sociology at the University of California, Berkeley, when Japanese Americans were ordered to evacuate the restricted military zone along the West Coast of the United States. Kikuchi's viewpoint is detached and sometimes sarcastic. A troubled childhood resulted in his being raised apart from both his family and the Japanese American community, and he felt some trepidation about rejoining his family and living among other Japanese Americans. Nevertheless, the entries indicate that Kikuchi developed a new appreciation for his family and the community. He wrote these diary entries while being interned with his family at the Tanforan racetrack south of San Francisco. Many Japanese Americans lived temporarily at makeshift camps like these before going to the more permanent relocation centers inland.

SOURCE. Charles Kikuchi, *The Kikuchi Diary: Chronicle from an American Concentration Camp*, University of Illinois Press, 1973, pp. 51–56, 61–63. Copyright © 1973 by the Board of Trustees of the University of Illinois. Used with permission of the University of Illinois Press.

April 30, 1942, Berkeley

Today is the day that we are going to get kicked out of Berkeley. It certainly is degrading. I am down here in the control station and I have nothing to do so I am jotting down these notes! The Army Lieutenant over there doesn't want any of the photographers to take pictures of these miserable people waiting for the Greyhound bus because he thinks that the American public might get a sympathetic attitude towards them.

I'm supposed to see my family at Tanforan [a racetrack in San Bruno, California, used as a temporary relocation center] as Jack [a friend] told me to give the same family number. I wonder how it is going to be living with them as I haven't done this for years and years? I should have gone over to San Francisco and evacuated with them, but I had a last final to take. I understand that we are going to live in the horse stalls. I hope that the Army has the courtesy to remove the manure first.

This morning I went over to the bank to close my account and the bank teller whom I have never seen before solemnly shook my hand and he said, "Goodbye, have a nice time." I wonder if that isn't the attitude of the American people? They don't seem to be bitter against us, and I certainly don't think I am any different from them. That General [John L.] De Witt certainly gripes my ass because he has been listening to the Associated Farmers [a group that resented Japanese American competition] too much.

Oh, oh, there goes a "thing" in slacks and she is taking pictures of that old Issei lady with a baby. She says she is the official photographer, but I think she ought to leave these people alone. The Nisei around here don't seem to be so sad. They look like they are going on a vacation. They are all gathered around the bulletin board to find out the exact date of their departure. "When are you leaving?" they are saying to one another. Some of those old Issei men must have gone on a binge last night because they smell like *sake*.

Mitch [a friend] just came over to tell us that I was going on the last bus out of Berkeley with him. Oh, how lucky I am! The Red Cross lady just told me that she would send a truck after my baggage and she wants the phone number. I never had a phone in that dump on Haste Street.

> The Issei smile even now though they are leaving with hearts full of sorrow. But the Nisei around here seem pretty bold and their manners are brazen.

I have a queer sensation and it doesn't seem real. There are smiling faces all around me and there are long faces and gloomy faces too. All kinds of Japanese and Caucasian faces around this place. Soon they will be neurotic cases. Wang [a friend] thinks that he has an empty feeling in his stomach and I told him to go get a hamburger upstairs because the Church people are handing out free food. I guess this is a major catastrophe so I guess we deserve some free concessions.

The Church people around here seem so nice and full of consideration saying, "Can we store your things?" "Do you need clothes?" "Sank you," the Issei smile even now though they are leaving with hearts full of sorrow. But the Nisei around here seem pretty bold and their manners are brazen. They are demanding service. I guess they are taking advantage of their college educations after all. "The Japs are leaving, hurrah, hurrah!" some little kids are yelling down the street but everybody ignores them. Well, I have to go up to the campus and get the results of my last exam and will barely be able to make it back here in time for the last bus. God, what a prospect to look forward to living among all those Japs!

May 3, 1942—Sunday

The whole family pitched in to build our new home at Tanforan. We raided the clubhouse and tore off the linoleum from the bar table and put it on our floor so that it now looks rather homelike. Takeshi [Tom] [a

brother] works pretty hard for a little guy and makes himself useful, but the gals are not so useful. They'd rather wander around looking for the boys. However, they pitched in and helped clean up the new messhall so that we could have our meals there instead of walking all the way over to the clubhouse. It's about 11:00 now and everyone has gone to bed. You can hear the voices all the way down the barracks—everything sounds so clear. Tom just stepped out to water his "victory garden." The community spirit is picking up rapidly and everyone seems willing to pitch in. They had a meeting tonight to get volunteers for cooks and waiters at the new messhall and this was done without difficulty. Rules were also made for each barracks such as radio off at 10:00 and not too many lights so that the fuse would not set overload.

We have only been here three days, but it already seems like weeks. Everyone here has fallen into the regular routine, without any difficult adjustments except Pop, who was a problem child this morning. He got mad because be was not getting the proper food [for his diabetic condition] so he went off by himself and got lost.

There are still many problems to be solved such as heating, cleaner dishes, more variety of foods, recreational, and other social problems, but they will most likely be settled in time.

I saw a soldier in a tall guardhouse near the barbed wire fence and did not like it because it reminds me of a concentration camp. I am just wondering what the effects will be on the Japanese so cut off from the world like this. Within the confines of Tanforan our radios and papers are the only touch with reality. I hardly know how the war is going now, and it is so significant that the Allied forces win even though that will not mean that democracy will by any means be perfect or even justified. The whole post war period is going to be something terrific. Sometimes I feel like a foreigner in

Photo on previous page: According to an internee's diary, the mess hall was a source of tension in the camp as people complained about the food. (Time & Life Pictures/Getty Images.)

this camp hearing so much Japanese although our family uses English almost exclusively.

Taro [Katayana, an acquaintance] lives up in the Men's dormitory, the majority of whom are Issei, and he has a big American flag over his head for identification. I wonder what the Issei think of this. I haven't heard any talk about a "Japanese victory" although it must go on. You just can't change a group overnight, especially in the face of the fact that the Japanese have been so discriminated against in this state—witness the long history of anti-orientalism.

> From an individual standpoint our family has not lost anything. We have been drawn close together as a group and everyone seems cheerful enough.

We are planning to get the paper underway as soon as possible. It is needed now as a "morale raiser" and also for the information service that it could render. With 4000 more people coming in next week, the confusion may grow greater.

From an individual standpoint our family has not lost anything. We have been drawn close together as a group and everyone seems cheerful enough. Jack [brother] is straining a bit because of Helen [Jack's girlfriend], I suppose, but he doesn't say too much. I tried to get him interested in the Medical Department here, but he was not too enthusiastic. He did show an interest in the library though. Tom and Miyako [sister] are having a grand vacation. I hope they do not delay in setting up an efficient school system—education is so important for the future.

May 4, 1942—Monday

There are such varied reactions to the whole thing: some are content and thankful; others gush "sank you" but are full of complaints within their own circles. Still others are bolder and come right out with it. We thought that we would not have any dinner tonight because the cooks went on a strike. They really are overworked—preparing 3000 meals. Then there have been considerable "personality difficulties." The battle for prestige here is terrific—everyone wants to be a somebody, it seems—any kind of work will do as long as they get the official badges that distinguish them. The waiters also joined the strike because they only have 1000 dishes to feed 3000 people and they really have to get them out in a rush. I saw one Issei dishwasher slap a Nisei girl because she complained that the cups were so dirty. Their nerves are on edge in the cooking division because they are the target for many complaints when it really is not their fault. They are going to open up the new messhalls for sure tomorrow so a great deal of the overload rush will be cut down. The electricians are also griped because they have to replace so many fuses. The wiring system in the stables is very poor and with all the extra lights needed, the system has broken down. Because of the cold, many of the people use cooking heaters to keep warm with. They brought in 50 kerosene heaters today for the aged, ill, and the babies, but this is by no means sufficient.

Oh, I sure could go for a hamburger now: the big juicy kind. I've eaten so much canned food the past week that it becomes tasteless. Many of the boys are worried about being fed saltpeter because they think it will ruin their manhood.

A contrasting reaction is the number of victory gardens that are being planted; these industrious Japanese! They just don't seem to know how to take it easy—they've worked so hard all of their lives that they just can't stand idleness—or waste. They are so concerned that water is not left running or that electricity is not being wasted. Today many of the smaller family units were asked to move to make room for the new evacuees and they certainly did squawk. Here they have their places all fixed up nice and cozy and then they have to start all over again. But they will take it without too much fuss. I wonder if it is because they feel thankful for any treatment that they get regardless of what it is or whether they still are full of unnecessary fears about how the government is going to treat them. Sometimes I get tired of hearing all these "sank you's" which certainly is not the real feeling in so many cases. . . .

May 7, 1942—Thursday

There are all different types of Japanese in camp. Many of the young Nisei are quite Americanized and have nice personalities. They smile easily and are not inhibited in their actions. They have taken things in stride and their sole concern is to meet the other sex, have dances so that they can jitterbug, get a job to make money for "cokes," and have fun in general. Many are using the evacuation to break away from the strict control of parental rule.

> The young Nisei . . . have taken things in stride and their sole concern is to meet the other sex, have dances so that they can jitterbug, get a job to make money for 'cokes,' and have fun in general.

Other Nisei think more in terms of the future. They want to continue their education in some sort of "career" study and be successes. The background which they come from is very noticeable: their parents were better educated and had businesses. One Nisei girl was telling me today about how Grant Avenue [San Francisco] art goods stores were sold out. They used a lot of Nisei girls and those stores that were in control of Caucasian hands paid twice as much in salary as those owned by Japanese. Many of the shrewd Jewish businessmen bought the whole store out and they got a lot of old stock out of warehouses and sold them in the evacuation sale. They used the Japanese stores as a front to unload this junk on the public. The art goods stores, even Chinese, are having a difficult time because they cannot get any more stock in from the Orient. I asked the girl what her father expected to do after the war and she said that he and his wife would probably be forced to leave this country, but the girl expects to get married and stay here.

Made me feel sort of sorry for Pop tonight. He has his three electric clippers hung up on the wall and Tom has built him a barrel chair for the barber seat. It's a bit pathetic when he so tenderly cleans off the clippers after using them; oiling, brushing, and wrapping them up so carefully. He probably realizes that he no longer controls the family group and rarely exerts himself so that there is little family conflict as far as he is concerned. What a difference from about 15 years ago when I was a kid. He used to be a perfect terror and dictator. I think most of us have inherited this tendency to be dominant, except perhaps Alice [sister]. She is not too aggressive and she would perhaps make some fellow a nice wife. She has worked hard for the past four years and helped support the family so that now she is more or less inclined to be a little queenish. Alice has never gone beyond her high school level of friends and this is the type that she goes around with now—nothing wrong in that, I suppose, but I do think that she should be more advanced than to confine herself with Emiko's and Bette's [sisters] "jitterbug" friends.

Emiko is very boy-conscious also and her idea of life right now is good clothes, plenty of boy friends, and jitterbug music. She will probably get over the stage soon. She gets along well with the fellows and is capable of adjustments to any circumstances.

Bette is also getting at that age and sometimes she feels that Jack and I don't approve of it so she hesitates a bit at times in approving all of these light activities. She seems to be more responsible than the other two and she certainly has a clever sense of humor. She, too, is getting boystruck. Right now, she worries about her weight so that she makes Miyako or Tom walk around the track with her for the "exercise."

Mom is taking things in stride. I have a suspicion that she rather enjoys the whole thing. It certainly is a change from her former humdrum life. She dyed her hair today, and Pop made some comment that she shouldn't try to act so young. One thing about these stables is that it does cut down the amount of "nagging" because people can overhear everything that is said.

A Married Couple, Separated by Internment, Tries to Maintain Hope

Hanaye and Iwao Matsushita

The following selection consists of an exchange of letters between a married Japanese American couple from Seattle, Washington. After an initial detention at the Puyallup Fairgrounds south of Seattle, the two were separated. Husband Iwao went to the Fort Missoula Internment Camp in Montana, while wife Hanaye was taken to the Minidoka Camp in Idaho. The letters are unusual accounts of the camps since Iwao and Hanaye were Issei, or first-generation Japanese immigrants who had been prevented from achieving US citizenship. Most accounts of the camps were written by younger, second-generation Nisei, who were largely American

SOURCE. Hanaye Matsushita and Iwao Matsushita, "Part Two: Wartime Correspondence," *Imprisoned Apart: The World War II Correspondence of an Issei Couple*, University of Washington Press, 1997, pp. 164–169. Copyright © 1997 by University of Washington Press. Reproduced by permission.

citizens. The letters reflect many Japanese traditions: Hanaye does not address her letters by name but rather to "My dear husband" in the Japanese manner and is always polite and graceful, even when talking about camp guards. Her letters also show a love for and awareness of nature, and one of Iwao's includes poems in a terse Japanese style inspired by the camps. While many of the letters simply refer to the details of daily life, they also suggest hardship and suffering.

Aug. 6 [1942], morning

My dear husband:

Yesterday I received your letter of the first. Thank you. I'm glad to hear that you are doing well. I've enjoyed the dry pressed flowers enclosed in the last letter and cried with nostalgia remembering the fun days we've had. . . .

Every day has been busy. I just finished cleaning the bathroom and now hastily pick up my pen to write. I'm behind in responding to you because my left eye has worsened and makes it hard to write. It's probably just age, so don't worry. I told Uncle about it, but he ignores my complaints, so I cling to God. Most days we don't see each other all day long. I look forward to living by myself after the move.

> Those from whom I wouldn't have expected anything have been very generous.

Until now I've used Uncle's family number, but I'll get my own soon. He continues to demonstrate the usual disregard for anything and everything. I've finally gotten it through my head that he's a completely unreliable person, but don't worry, I live with God.

Those from whom I wouldn't have expected anything have been very generous, while I've grown apart from friends with whom I used to be in contact. Now I only see them once in a while. It's comforting having Aunt Kaneko living nearby.

Two days ago I received a $2.50 coupon book for the second time, and I'm thankful for the money since I am too weak to work. Uncle apparently received $15 or $16.

The morning of the 7th: Yesterday was so busy that I couldn't finish the letter so will continue writing today. The day of our move to Idaho approaches. We'll probably move around the 16th. I'm too busy to relax. I'm in charge of packing the bags. Uncle is always at the hospital. I'd prefer that he return home earlier in the evenings, but there's nothing I can do about it.

Writing a letter in English is difficult and it frustrates me that Uncle won't help me. Every morning I go to church to pray that you are well and that you'll return as soon as possible. . . .

My heart is racing; I'll put down my pen here.

Hana

Aug. 8, 1942

Dear Hanaye,

I've begun to feel the chill in the mornings and nights of the Missoula [Montana] highlands. Autumn must be just around the corner. The chilly morning makes me want to bask in the morning sunshine, but it gets quite warm in the afternoons. Yesterday as I was teaching my class, I could feel the perspiration running down my back.

I see from my friends' letters that the time is getting near for those of you at Puyallup [Washington] to be moving out to another camp. Even though it's been only three months in your temporary quarters, it must have been like being settled, and I know it must be hard for you to make a move again.

The population of this camp has diminished a lot, and it has become very quiet. Food has improved, and there's a movie every Tuesday and Saturday afternoon. They say we'll be allowed to go down to the Missoula River on Wednesdays starting next week. I have a feeling, though, that this won't last for long.

To give you an idea of the kind of meals we are getting, here's what we had recently: *gomoku* [seasoned rice with vegetable slivers], veal cutlet, French fried potatoes, and jello. Quite a fancy meal. Occasionally our trays are adorned with lettuce and tomato, too. It's great. We cook our own *somen* and fish cakes.

> The room is cold
> my stroll outdoors.

> Buzzing wind cools
> an electric fan.

> I call, "come on"
> kitten scoots.

> Kittens two
> in the barrack loitering.

Health's first. Please give my regards to Doc. Also to your doctor neighbor. I'm sure you'll be in his care, too. Give them my thanks and regards.
    Iwao

Aug. 11, 1942

Dear Hanaye,
    I was greatly relieved after seeing your letter with the enclosed pressed flower. If, as you say, your vision is due to age, I wouldn't be concerned. But shouldn't you see the doctor in case there's something wrong?
    You must be in the midst of packing and looking after other matters readying for the move to Idaho. I apologize for the helpless situation I'm in and not being able to help you through this. Don't be overly concerned, be calm and collected, and make an effort to relax. I know this may be asking too much of you because you're such a hard worker, but it's for your health.

> "I apologize for the helpless situation I'm in and not being able to help you through this.

No matter what the circumstances, let us have faith in the Lord that He will protect us, and live our daily lives with gratitude. Although it's unnatural and painful to be separated for so long, there are others who are in similar straits. There are many in much more trying situations. I'd like to think that God is testing our faith and polishing our lives.

Kumasaka-san has asked me to thank you for looking after his family. Please relay my many thanks and regards to Kondo-san. Health comes first.

Iwao

Aug. 20, morning
Minidoka Relocation Center

My dear husband:

On the 15th we left Puyallup and arrived here around four in the afternoon on the 16th. The doctors will stay in Puyallup until the 28th or 29th of next month. Or, at the worst, they'll be sent somewhere else. I'm resigned to try living a bachelor's life. Aunt Kaneko and I are doing well living together. I owe a lot to her. Two or three single women will move in nearby since there are not enough living quarters to go around. . . .

It's unendurably hot and dusty, though eventually I'll get used to it. My body is weak and can only stand so much. I pray to God for strength and tolerance. At times like this I wish day and night for your quick return. . . .

I have many things to tell you, but in the afternoons I am worthless because of the horrible heat. When I dwell on this situation, I have suicidal feelings, but I've got to keep myself together until your return. I imagine you're also experiencing rough times. I have come to understand what it's like to live alone in this world. People tease me, calling me the Montana widow. . . .

I can hear the violent winds blowing across the wide plains. In the distance I hear the sound of the sagebrush blowing in the wind, rattlesnakes, and the howling of coyotes.

I'm thankful to this country that we can live here in safety. The soldiers stand guard day and night. I shed tears of sympathy for them standing in the scorching afternoon heat and the evenings that are so cold as to require lighting a fire, for each soldier is someone's son. At night a crescent moon shines brightly, the grandiosity of nature brings tears to my eyes. I need to focus my mind on something. I'll ponder God's benevolence.

> "The soldiers stand guard day and night. I shed tears of sympathy for them standing in the scorching afternoon heat and the evenings that are so cold."

The house we are living in now is built for winter and equipped with a new coal stove so we won't die of the cold. We eat at the cafeteria.

Our boxes have yet to arrive, so we have no tables or chairs. I am writing this letter on my lap. We should be settled in a few days. I anxiously await your next letter and pray that your day of return comes soon. Take care of your health. I'll write again.

Hana

Aug. 25, 1942
To Mrs. Hanaye Matsushita
1-2-C, Minidoka WRA
Eden, Idaho

Dear Hanaye,

I was happy to receive word of your safe move. I studied the map the other day and learned that you were located far south of us. I imagine it's very hot there. Once you've become used to it, it shouldn't be too bad. Take care of your health, that's of the primary importance.

The number in this camp is gradually diminishing as people are transferred or released to the "outside." It probably won't be long now. My fate is entirely unknown.

Be prepared for the worst, should that happen, [CEN-SORED] is being transferred, too.

As I have said many times, if you remember that there are many others who are worse off, we'll be able to give thanks no matter what may befall us. If we trust in the Lord, even if we are left alone in the wilderness, we'll not feel any loneliness.

With the lessening population, my chore days come almost daily. However, meals continue to get better. For example, for breakfast we have hot cakes, corn flakes, bologna, and pears, and for dinner miso salmon, cucumber pickles, miso pork, and mixed rice. It's sumptuous. We have movies twice a week. I was reminded of the old days when I saw *Sun Valley Serenade* and *Charley's Aunt*.

Reports from other camps indicate that apparently there aren't places that are as good as Missoula. No word can describe the air of the highlands. Snow is still left on Mount Lolo. To be sure, they say there are lots of fireflies in the forest of Louisiana.

My regards to Aunt Kaneko. I'll write again. Please take care.

Iwao

Recalling the Camps More than Fifty Years Later

Reiko Oshima Komoto

The Japanese Americans who lived in the internment camps were changed by the experience and, for the most part, could still recall them clearly years later. In the following selection, Reiko Oshima Komoto recalls how, at the age of ten, she was evacuated from her Northern California home in 1942. The family's first destination was the temporary relocation center at the Tanforan racetrack near San Francisco. Eventually, the family ended up at Topaz in Utah, one of the largest of the internment camps. In addition to describing the details of everyday life, the author explains that one way out of the camps was to move eastward, away from the West Coast. Her older brothers and sisters did so, resulting in a temporary breakup of the family. She also provides brief comments

SOURCE. Reiko Oshima Komoto, "Japanese Internment Camps: A Personal Account," uwec.edu, March, 1997. Reproduced by permission. Copyright © by Reiko Oshima Komoto. Reprinted by permission of the author.

about how uncertain she felt after leaving the camp and expresses
hope that the lessons of the camps remain clear.

My name is Reiko Oshima Komoto. I was born in San Lorenzo, California, in 1932.
Regarding my internment years, my recollections of fifty-five years ago are fragmentary. It may be subconsciously on purpose: it was not a good experience.

The family consisted of Father, Mother, four boys, and three girls; and we lived in Oakland, California. Father and Mother were residents of California for twenty-one years at the time. Most of the children were attending school when the order to relocate all Japanese Americans from the West Coast was issued on March 1942. We were sent to Tanforan Race Track (an assembly center) in San Bruno, California, with only what we could carry in clothing and personal possessions. All radios and cameras were confiscated. Furniture and household goods were stored in our next door neighbor's basement and never retrieved.

From California to Utah

Our sleeping quarters consisted of two white washed horse stalls. All bathrooms, dining hall, and similar rooms were located in other buildings. School was held in the dining room with all grades and dining tables in place of desks. We stayed at Tanforan Race Track for probably about six months before we were sent by train (only a few seats were available) to Topaz, Utah. Topaz was located in the Sevier Desert, near the small town of Delta, Utah. As a consequence I missed the flowers, trees, and green plants that grew so abundantly in California. Can you imagine being thrilled to see a living, green tree?!

> " I missed the flowers, trees, and green plants that grew so abundantly in California. "

Topaz consisted of blocks; how many I don't recall, but the total number of people was approximately 8,300. Each block contained two rows of eight, tar-papered barracks, one-story, twenty by one hundred feet. An H-shaped building in the middle of the block contained a laundry room, separate bathrooms for males and females. All shower and toilet stalls were without doors or curtains. Each block also had a separate building for meals. I remember waiting in line to receive our food and lots of organ meats (kidney, liver and heart) being served. Food on the most part was not good depending on the cook's culinary skills and groceries allotted. Our sleeping quarters consisted of two large rooms (approximately 20' x 25'); metal cots, and army blankets. There was a pot bellied stove for heating. I saw snow for the first time but don't remember it collecting on the ground for any length of time. I remember sand covering the room after storms (resembling miniature tornadoes).

One barrack for the whole camp was used as a store; another as a movie theater, and one as a library. The library was quite a distance from our block, but walking was the only alternative since cars were not allowed. The neighbor across the street somehow managed to make a pool with local fish swimming in it. How he obtained the cement and fish, I have no clue. Somehow I acquired a horned toad as a pet. I don't believe pets were allowed, though an elderly man was shot trying to retrieve his dog that got too close to the fence.

In the beginning, guards with questionable intelligence manned the towers around the fenced camp. However, even if one could escape there was no place to go in the desert, in Utah, on foot, with an Asian face. Eventually, the guards were gone but no one tried to escape. A person could legitimately leave the camp if a person relocated to any place but the West Coast.

Jobs in the camp paid from twelve (for women) to nineteen dollars per month. Your occupational status

Photo on previous page: The Tanforan Race Track in San Bruno, California, served as temporary housing for many Japanese internees before they were sent to more permanent camps. (**Associated Press.**)

before being interned had no bearing on your pay. Medical doctors were paid nineteen dollars, while my Father received sixteen dollars for inspecting the camps' bathrooms.

Work and School

School was held in designated barracks. I learned formation marching, volleyball, and basketball, but I have no recollection of being taught the three R's; therefore, I have gaps in my formal education. One of my teachers had an eighth grade educational background. I have fond memories of one teacher who stressed initiative, and her parties were memorable. I'll always remember the punch she made from grape jam. All my teachers were Caucasian though I'm sure there must have been Japanese teachers with teaching degrees. The teachers at Tanforan Race Track were Japanese who were probably college students. Piano lessons were available but after several lessons I quit since I could not practice on a piano. Only a few pianos were available in the whole camp. A table wasn't a very acceptable substitute. I did have a few vocal lessons. I managed to win a talent contest and sang solos at church services while in camp. The one life-long activity I acquired in camp was the love of reading. Consequently, I became a voracious reader as a child and hope to renew that activity when I retire.

> Adjustment to life outside the camp was difficult. I was afraid a great deal of the time.

My oldest brother left camp to work in a factory in Cleveland, Ohio. My two sisters moved to St. Paul, Minnesota, to work as maids in a private home. All my brothers eventually moved to Minneapolis, Minnesota. The rest of us joined them when the camp was closed in 1945. Remarkably my oldest brother was able to purchase a home.

Out of camp, school was foreign in many ways, including the usual things a student encounters going from elementary to junior high school. I also had the difficulty of entering after the school year had already started, and I missed many of the subjects that should have been presented from 3rd to 6th grade. I was afraid someone would create a scene and hatefully call me a Jap!!!

I recall trying to walk on ice and hitting my head after a fall and falling down a few more times before arriving at school. I still have a scar on my head as a reminder. Adjustment to life outside the camp was difficult. I was afraid a great deal of the time. I didn't want to encounter incidents of prejudice. I became a timid and introverted person, which I've overcome as I've aged.

Hopefully, people will learn from this unfortunate episode in our history. People are people; judge them as individuals, not by race, color, or creed. No Japanese American was ever tried for espionage.

CHRONOLOGY

1790   A Naturalization Act limits US citizenship to immigrants who are "free white persons."

1868   The first Japanese immigrants begin to arrive in the then-independent Kingdom of Hawaii.

The US government ratifies the Fourteenth Amendment to the Constitution, which guarantees citizenship to all people born on American soil.

1869   The first Japanese immigrants reach the United States. They form an agricultural community in California.

1882   Numbers of Japanese immigrants to both the United States and Hawaii increase after the Chinese Exclusion Act ends immigration from China.

1898   Hawaii becomes a territory of the United States. Among its population are more than fifty thousand Japanese immigrants.

1906   Anti-Japanese sentiment becomes vocal in California, notably in San Francisco, where some Japanese children are excluded from public schools.

1907   President Theodore Roosevelt ends the ban of Japanese school children in San Francisco, but the US government forbids the entrance of new Japanese laborers to the mainland unless they are the immediate relatives of people already in the United States.

1908   In the "Gentlemen's Agreement," the Japanese govern-
          ment agrees to grant no new passports to laborers who
          want to go to the United States.

1908–1920 Many Japanese laborers in Hawaii and on the mainland
          enter into arranged marriages with "picture brides," thus
          enabling them to start families in the United States.

1924   A broad Immigration Act bans any further newcomers
          from Japan.

1937   Imperial Japan invades China.

1940   Imperial Japan occupies French Indochina, resulting
          in a significant rise in tensions between Japan and the
          United States.

1941   October: The US Army begins training a small group
          of Nisei, or second-generation Japanese Americans, as
          language specialists and translators.

          November: A US government investigation concludes
          that there is little reason to question the loyalty of
          Japanese Americans in Hawaii or on the mainland.

          December 7: Imperial Japan attacks the US naval base
          at Pearl Harbor, Hawaii. The United States declares war
          on Japan the next day.

          December 11: The US government arrests about two
          thousand Issei, or first-generation Japanese Americans.
          Most are considered to be community leaders in some
          capacity.

1942   January: The US attorney general, Francis Biddle,
          begins the process of establishing "military areas" on
          the West Coast of the United States.

February 4: Biddle permits the enforcement of curfews in California.

February 14: Lieutenant General John L. DeWitt, head of the Western Defense Command, officially recommends the removal of all Japanese people from vital military areas along the West Coast.

February 19: In Executive Order 9066, President Franklin D. Roosevelt grants DeWitt, or other relevant military officials, the right to both establish military areas and remove from those areas any people thought to be suspicious.

March 2: General DeWitt issues public proclamations designating the western parts of California, Oregon, and Washington and the southern areas of Arizona as special "military zones."

March 18: The War Relocation Authority is established to manage the process of the relocation of Japanese Americans as well as to govern any eventual relocation centers.

March 22: The first large group of evacuated Japanese, from Los Angeles, go to Manzanar, eventually the site of a large internment camp in the inland California desert.

March–April: Organized evacuations continue. Many Japanese are sent first to converted horse racetracks such as Santa Anita or Tanforan in California or to similar facilities such as the Puyallup Fairgrounds in Washington.

May 5: Gordon Hirabayashi, a University of Washington student, refuses to obey a curfew order and turns himself in to authorities.

May–October: Internment Camps open at Tule Lake in Northern California, Minidoka in Utah, Heart Mountain in Wyoming, Poston and Gila River in Arizona, Granada in Colorado, and Rohwer and Jerome in Arkansas.

July 20: Evacuees who are Nisei, and therefore US citizens, are granted permission to leave the camps to work at jobs in inland areas.

1943   February: President Roosevelt authorizes the formation of the 442nd Regimental Combat Team, made up almost entirely of Japanese Americans. Later combined with the US Army's 100th Battalion, made up of Nisei from Hawaii, it is intended for use in Europe against Nazi Germany.

All internment camp residents seventeen years of age or older are given a loyalty questionnaire. Its primary purpose is to determine which Nisei should be eligible for military service. The questionnaire is also used to identify potentially "disloyal" Japanese Americans so they can be segregated.

June: The US Supreme Court decides that Gordon Hirabayashi was guilty of a violation of legitimate curfew rules in 1942, thereby upholding the right of the US government to establish special rules for particular ethnic groups in a time of war.

July: Those whose responses to the loyalty questionnaire were deemed "unsatisfactory" are sent to the Tule Lake camp. Disturbances there later result in the camp being placed under military control.

1944   June: The camp at Jerome, Arkansas, is the first to be closed. Its remaining internees are sent to other camps.

The Fair Play Committee takes shape at Wyoming's Heart Mountain Camp. Its members refuse to serve in the US armed forces, even if they are drafted, on the grounds that the relocation orders violated their rights as citizens. Many are eventually arrested as draft evaders.

December 17: The relocation orders of 1942 are revoked, effective January 2, 1945. Japanese Americans are now free to return to the West Coast.

December 18: The War Relocation Authority announces that the internment camps will all be closed by June 30, 1946.

1945 May 8: World War II in Europe ends.

August 15: Japan surrenders following the United States' dropping of atomic weapons on the cities of Hiroshima and Nagasaki.

October–December: Aside from Tule Lake, all the remaining internment camps are closed.

1946 March: Tule Lake closes.

1948 Japanese Americans are given the ability to file claims against the government for property losses during the years of relocation. Before the program stops, about $31 million is paid out, far less than the value of lost property.

1952 New immigration laws allow the Issei and other Asian immigrants to apply for US citizenship.

1959 Hawaii becomes the fiftieth US state.

1970   The movement calling for official apologies and redress for wartime internees is begun by Nisei and Sansei (third-generation) activists.

1976   President Gerald Ford officially rescinds 1942's Executive Order 9066.

1980   President Jimmy Carter establishes the Committee on Wartime Relocation and Internment of Civilians, adding momentum to calls for redress and compensation.

1987   After a legal battle, Gordon Hirabayashi's 1943 Supreme Court conviction is overturned.

1988   President Ronald Reagan signs a new Civil Liberties Act, providing payments of $20,000 to each surviving internee as well as issuing a formal apology.

1992   The Manzanar Camp is named an official US historical landmark. Efforts are soon begun to give similar status to other camps.

FOR FURTHER READING

Books

Lyn Crost, *Honor by Fire: Japanese Americans at War in Europe and the Pacific*. Novato, CA: Presido Press, 1994.

Roger Daniels, *Concentration Camps North America: Japanese in the United States and Canada During World War II*. Malabar, FL: Robert E. Krieger, 1981.

Roger Daniels, Sandra C. Taylor, and Harry L Kitano, eds., *Japanese Americans: From Relocation to Redress*. Seattle: University of Washington Press, 1991.

Deborah Gesensway and Mindy Roseman, *Beyond Words: Images from America's Concentration Camps*. Ithaca, NY: Cornell University Press, 1987.

Bill Hosokawa, *Nisei: The Quiet Americans*. Boulder: University Press of Colorado, 2002.

Lawson Inada, ed., *Only What We Could Carry: The Japanese American Internment Experience*. Berkeley: Heyday Books, 2000.

Peter Irons, *The Courage of Their Convictions*. New York: Free Press, 1988.

Thomas James, *Exile Within: The Schooling of Japanese Americans 1942–1945*. Cambridge, MA: Harvard University Press, 1987; New York: Bedford/St. Martin's, 2000.

Dillon S. Myer, *Uprooted Americans: The Japanese Americans and the War Relocation Authority During World War II*. Tucson: University of Arizona Press, 1971.

David Neiwert, *Strawberry Days: How Internment Destroyed a Japanese American Community*. New York: Palgrave MacMillan, 2005.

David J. O'Brien and Stephen S. Fugita, *The Japanese American Experience*. Bloomington: Indiana University Press, 1991.

John Okada, *No-No Boy*. Rutherford, VT: Charles E. Tuttle, 1957.

Michael O'Tunnell and George W. Chilcoat, *The Children of Topaz: The Story of a Japanese American Internment Camp*. New York: Holiday House, 1996.

Greg Robinson, *By Order of the President: FDR and the Internment of Japanese Americans*. Cambridge, MA: Harvard University Press, 2001.

Monica Sone, *Nisei Daughter*. Seattle: University of Washington Press, 1953.

John Tateishi, *And Justice for All: An Oral History of the Japanese American Detention Camps*. New York: Random House, 1984.

Periodicals

Mike Barber, "Hirabayashi Was One Who Wouldn't Give In," *Seattle Post-Intelligencer*, November 26, 1999.

Alison Bell, "Santa Anita Played a Role in WWII Internment," *Los Angeles Times*, November 8, 2009.

Sharon Boswell and Lorraine McConaghy, "Abundant Dreams Diverted," *Seattle Times*, June 23, 1996.

Tiffany Carney, "Images Tell Story of Interned Japanese Americans," *San Jose Mercury News*, October 21, 2010.

Ryan Kim, "Japanese American Hero Remembered: Fred Korematsu Fought WWII Internment," *San Francisco Chronicle*, April 17, 2005.

The Kitchen Sisters, "Weenie Royale: Food and the Japanese Internment," Npr.org, December 2007.

Kevin Allen Leonard, "Is That What We Fought For? Japanese Americans and Racism in California: The Impact of World War II," *Western Historical Quarterly*, 21 no. 4, November 1990.

David Margolick, "Japanese American Judges Reflect on Internment," *New York Times*, May 19, 1995.

Patti Murphy, "Memories of Minidoka: Japanese-Americans revisit southern Idaho's internment camp," *Boise Weekly*, May 5, 2010.

Annie Nakao, "Haunting Memories of Japanese Internment," *San Francisco Chronicle*, February 18, 2003.

National Park Service, "The War Relocation Centers of World War II: When Fear Was Stronger than Justice," Nps.gov.

Gary Y. Okihiro, "Tule Lake under Martial Law: A Study in Japanese Resistance," *Journal of Ethnic Studies*, 5, Fall 1977.

Howard Pankratz, "Sites of WWII Japanese-American Internment Camps Get Grants," *Denver Post*, December 29, 2010.

Dinitia Smith, "Photographs of an Episode that Lives in Infamy," *New York Times*, November 6, 2006.

Paul Spickard, "The Nisei Assume Power: The Japanese Citizens League, 1941–1942," *Pacific Historical Review*, 52 no. 2, May 1983.

Sandra C. Taylor, "Leaving the Concentration Camps: Japanese American Resettlement in Utah and the Intermountain West," *Pacific Historical Review*, 60 no. 2, May 1991.

Brian Thornton, "Heroic editors in short supply during Japanese Internment," *Newspaper Research Journal*, Spring 2002.

Mark Weber, "The Japanese Camps in California," *Journal of Historical Review*, Spring 1980.

Websites

Densho (www.densho.org). Devoted to preserving the memory of the internment experience, this website offers historical narratives, a learning center, and a large digital archive of interviews and other resources.

Information on Manzanar (www.manzanar.com). One of several websites devoted to particular internment camps, emphasizing both their histories and the importance of memory and preservation. Most of these sites offer interactive experiences and the opportunity for viewers to send additions. See also www.topazmuseum.org, www.tulelake.org. www.minidoka.org, and www.postoncamp.blogspot.com.

Japanese American Citizens League (www.jacl.org). This website is maintained by the oldest Japanese American organization in the United States. It provides links to articles and other historical information on the internment camps.

Japanese American National Museum (www.janm.org). A website maintained by the largest museum in the United States devoted to the Japanese American experience. It offers educational outreach and an archive of many materials dedicated to the internment camps.

Japanese American Veterans Association (www.javadc.org). This website, devoted to Japanese American veterans of the US armed services, offers material on those Nisei who served during World War II.

INDEX